Gregory van Dyk has travelled widely in the USA investigating evidence, interviewing witnesses and meeting key people in this field. His research is truly impressive. He lives in London and Colorado.

THE ALIEN FILES

THE SECRETS OF EXTRATERRESTRIAL ENCOUNTERS AND ABDUCTIONS

Gregory van Dyk

ELEMENT

Shaftesbury, Dorset • Rockport, Massachussets
Melbourne, Victoria

© Element Books Limited 1997
Text © Gregory van Dyk 1997

First published in Great Britain in 1997 by
Element Books Limited
Shaftesbury, Dorset SP7 8BP

Published in the USA in 1997 by
Element Books, Inc.
PO Box 830, Rockport, MA 01966

Published in Australia in 1997 by
Element Books and distributed by
Penguin Books Australia Ltd
487 Maroondah Highway,
Ringwood, Victoria 3134

Cover design by Max Fairbrother
Design by Roger Lightfoot
Typeset by Intype London Ltd
Printed and bound in Great Britain by
Biddles Ltd, Guildford & Kings Lynn and in the USA by
Courier Westford Inc, Westford, MA

British Library Cataloguing in Publication
data available

Library of Congress Cataloging in Publication
Van Dyk, Gregory.
    The alien files : the secrets of extra-terrestrial encounters and
abductions / Gregory van Dyk.
        p.   cm.
    Includes bibliographical references and index.
    ISBN 1-86204-135-0 (hardcover : alk. paper)
    1. Human-alien encounters.   2. Alien abduction.   I. Title.
BF2050.V26   1997
001.942—dc21   97-30188
                                                                     CIP

ISBN 1 86204 135 0

CONTENTS

ACKNOWLEDGEMENTS

I am especially grateful to Ian Fenton for his invaluable support and friendship, and to Matthew Cory of Element Books for his assistance in preparing this book for publication. I would like to record my thanks to Mary Aver for her spiritual guidance and help in clarifying my thinking about the chapters that deal with the spirit world. I am indebted to Catherine Ashman for her careful reading of the text and assisting my clarity of expression, and to Mark Hartman for participating in the creation of Zog.

I also wish to thank and acknowledge the following:

- Stanton Friedman for being an inspiration to all those interested in the subject, and for his photograph holding the latest MJ-12 material.
- Deon Crosby, Director of the International UFO Museum & Research Center (IUFOMRC) in Roswell, New Mexico, for the material about the museum and information about the Roswell Incident.
- Brian Zeiler for the information from *Have We Visitors From Outer Space?*
- Chris Rutkowski of the University of Manitoba, Winnipeg, Manitoba, Canada and UFOROM (UFO Research Organization of Manitoba) for permission to use information from his article 'Val Johnson: Encounter of the Decade'.
- Chris Lambright for his account of Sgt Lonnie Zamora's encounter near Socorro, New Mexico, and permission to reproduce his painting of the ovoid craft and the drawings

that he used to clarify the shape of the craft and the symbols witnessed by Lonnie Zamora.

- Dragonbane for permission to use his article 'An Alien Harvest: Evidence of Grey Origins and Reasons for Human Abduction'.
- Lyssa Royal Holt and Royal Priest Research for allowing me to quote from *Preparing for Contact* by Lyssa Royal and Keith Priest.
- Walt Guimbellot for permission to use text on sightings from his Wally World web site.
- Danny Brown for the compendium of sightings that he maintains on his home site on the Internet.
- Mark Williams and Melinda Leslie for their list of 52 common indicators shared by most abductees from their article 'Have you had alien encounters?'
- Crow and Raine for information about the Bentwaters Rendlesham Incident.
- Michael Corbin, Director of ParaNet Information Services for the USAF training manual.
- Brian Crissey and Pam Meyer of Blue Water Publishing for the drawings by Betty Andreasson Luca. These drawings have been reprinted from *The Andreasson Affair* by Raymond E Fowler, with permission of Wild Flower Press, copyrights 1979 and 1994 by Raymond E Fowler and Betty Andreasson.

INTRODUCTION

'Why don't UFOs just land on the White House lawn?'

'Why doesn't somebody bring back a tail-pipe that's dropped off one of them?'

'If they were real, there would at least be some small piece of physical evidence available for examination.'

'Abductions are just some kind of new altered dream state.'

'The laws of science don't allow spacecraft to manoeuvre in the way that observers describe.'

These are just some of the statements which are regularly made by sceptics of the UFO phenomenon, and which have now acquired the status of clichés. They betray a set of assumptions of which the speakers are seldom aware, namely, that the world works in precisely the way that they have come to believe. In this book I hope to expose some of the assumptions.

I endeavour to meet six broad objectives:

- to establish the reality of extraterrestrial visitors to our planet
- to examine evidence which suggests that our governments may not be telling us the whole truth
- to evaluate the abduction phenomenon and the questions that arise from the accounts of abductees
- to explore what we can learn about extraterrestrials from channelling and channellers;
- to examine the link between spirituality and extraterrestrial visitors
- to shake in whatever small way that I can the blind faith

that many of us have that scientific materialism can provide all the answers.

Much of the material that I use is already available in one form or another. The first part of my book is therefore essentially a review of accounts which will generally be familiar to committed ufologists and those with an interest in the subject. But I hope that my reappraisal will make an easy introduction to the subject for the uninitiated.

One of the best known UFO stories is what is known as the Roswell Incident. I have been astounded by the number of people who say, 'Oh Roswell, I know all about that', and then reveal their abysmal ignorance of the subject. Quite often the total extent of their knowledge is that the supposed UFO turned out to be a weather balloon. To those readers who think in this way, I have this plea – please read the story in chapter 2.

1

REALITY OR FANTASY?

THE TERRIBLE SECRET

In *Intruders*, Budd Hopkins tells a story from Walter Laqueur's book *The Terrible Secret* about the Holocaust. Despite details of the Nazis' systematic extermination of Jews having been made available to the wider world, few believed it to be true. Even when a Polish eyewitness, Jan Karski, told the prominent Judge Frankfurter about what he had witnessed first-hand, the judge was unable to believe him. This was not an account of what someone else had seen, but Karski's own sworn personal testimony. Judge Frankfurter's response was that he was not suggesting that Karski was not telling the truth, but that he was unable to believe him.

Who in their right mind would indeed have thought that the government of one of the most civilized nations would adopt a policy of genocide against 6 million people, including many of its own citizens. Had Germany not been defeated, the evidence would never have been presented by the world media and the disappearance of those people would still be a matter of public debate, even now, over 50 years after the event. A peace treaty with Germany, unthinkable as it may seem in retrospect, would very likely have encouraged other governments to collude in the cover-up.

It is equally possible that the US government is for its own reasons imposing a silence on the subject of extraterrestrial visitations, in conjunction with other governments. There is certainly a policy to suppress the facts, to discredit witnesses, and to prevent evidence from reaching the public domain.

A recently published secret US government manual on the subject declares unequivocally:

> MJ-12 [a US government committee responsible for policy towards UFOs] takes the subject of the UFOBs, Extraterrestrial Technology and Extraterrestrial Biological Entities very seriously and considers the entire subject to be a matter of the very highest national security. For that reason *everything relating to the subject has been assigned the very highest security classification* [my emphasis].

The document is published in Stanton Friedman's book *Top Secret/Majic*, to which I will refer again later. The debunkers who have already begun to suggest that the document is a forgery are somehow reminiscent of Judge Frankfurter, for whom the information was too unbearable to believe.

OUR REALITY IS DETERMINED BY OUR ASSUMPTIONS

The extent to which our view of reality is determined by our assumptions and by social convention rather than by evidence has always puzzled me. Most people appear to have very clear notions about what reality is. To my mind, there has always been room for doubt, and for a number of alternative possibilities. Perhaps if I had lived in Europe towards the end of the 16th century, I might have been burned at the stake with Giordano Bruno, who with Galileo believed that the earth was not the centre of the universe, contrary to the dogma of the Catholic Church.

In the modern world our assumptions are conditioned by the scientific establishment, whose unfettered belief is that everything can be explained, and what cannot be explained is not 'normal'. Hence the term 'paranormal', which is used to signify unacceptability, although this view is beginning to change as the stranglehold that scientific materialism has over our intellectual life is weakened.

The view that we may in fact be able to learn about the universe other than via the observation of material phenomena is beginning to gain credence. Intuition, insight and spiritual connection are beginning to gain some respectability as being able to teach us something about the universe – and about the extraterrestrial visitors knocking on our door.

Ufologists fall broadly into two camps: those who adopt the conventional approach and consider only the physical evidence of sightings of solid objects; and those who are prepared to explore non-physical ways to understand and communicate with the visitors. Hypnotic regression and channelling are two of the tools used by the more innovative ufologists trying to find out what is going on. My endeavour is to explore all of the means of gleaning information about our extraterrestrial visitors, without the intellectual handcuffs of prejudice and assumption.

The story of Zog, a two-dimensional creature

In order to open the door to the possibility that everything may not be exactly as it seems, I would like to tell a seemingly silly story, which may catch your imagination and help introduce my argument.

Consider the question of other dimensions. We regard ourselves as three-dimensional beings: forward–backward, left–right and up–down. But imagine how magical we would appear to a two-dimensional creature. Let me tell you about my two-dimensional friend Zog. He is profoundly sceptical when I tell him about my ability to negotiate the third dimension of height, or altitude. As far as he is concerned, the earth is flat and the sun moves across the sky. The rest is unsubstantiated speculation.

In order to demonstrate to Zog that other dimensions are possible, I show him a map of the USA and suggest that we both travel from Washington DC to Sacramento, using our own routes but keeping to the same speed. With a snort he tells me that the shortest distance between two points is a straight line, and he draws such a line between the two cities as his proposed route.

Both cities are just north of the 38th parallel at 38.54 and 38.35 degrees respectively. We agree to start our journey at 38.35 degrees, about 22 miles south of the centre of

Washington. Because Zog is two-dimensional, we will for the purposes of this journey ignore the undulations of mountains and valleys. There is only one altitude as far as he is concerned.

Keen to demonstrate his superiority by getting to Sacramento before me, Zog sets off immediately. He knows that, in order for me to arrive before him, I will at some point have to overtake him. This would appear to be a sound conclusion – indeed irrefutable – based on the assumptions of Zog's two-dimensional world.

What Zog is not aware of is that the surface of the earth is in fact curved, and that the map we looked at represents this fact. It is shown with curved lines of latitude, which bow downwards, following Magellan's 'great circle'.

My route, as far as the map is concerned is an arc. From a two-dimensional perspective, it appears to be a diversion, swinging way to the south of Zog's route apparent straight line. But it is in fact the more direct route, following the curvature of the earth, whereas it is Zog's route that is the diversion – a diversion of some 200 miles. So when he finally arrives, puffing his way into Sacramento and finds me sitting in Julie's Café waiting for him, it seems to him as extraordinary as if I have walked through the wall – in the same way that many extra-terrestrial creatures are reported to do.

Linear time and conventional thinking

Our total commitment to the idea of linear time is similar to Zog's commitment to his idea of to the quickest way to travel between two points. Psychics who are able to have access via another aspect of their being to both the future and the past seem both bizarre and magical. Time is a convention that remains as powerful as our commitment to a three-dimensional world in which the only reality is a material, physical one.

It is a common enough belief that we are not merely mind and body, but spirit beings composed of energy, manifested in material form in a human body. And as spirit beings we are able to access another dimension beyond the physical. But because of our traditional assumptions about the nature of our world, we find this idea absurd. By its very definition of what is and what is not real, the conventional mind defines other-dimensional experiences as bizarre, paranormal and extraordinary.

Once we acknowledge the limitations of conventional thinking, however, and begin to expand our horizon of possibilities, activities such as extrasensory perception (ESP), channelling and remote viewing become more acceptable and more understandable. But they take place in another dimension, from which we exclude ourselves by our absolute commitment to our limitations. Greater acknowledgement of these activities and skill in recognizing them would not only lead to greater understanding; it would also help us to differentiate between valid practitioners and the more dubious.

So why is it that some people see alien spacecraft flitting across our skies and others are selectively abducted for inspection and examination, yet these extraterrestrial visitors still remain elusive to the vast majority of us. Fifty years have passed since the Roswell Incident (*see* chapter 2), and the visitors have still not revealed themselves to the mass of humanity, other than by accident, unless they have found a way to live among us without being identified. The answer is that, if there *are* extraterrestrials with superhuman abilities, we would not know about them unless we had a higher-dimensional consciousness, in the same way as Zog was unable to comprehend my three-dimensional route because of his two-dimensional view.

ARE THE ALIENS SUPERIOR TO US?

The visitors appear to be vastly superior to us technologically; they might well be able to outgun us. The best military hardware appears to be powerless against them, even though the US military have succeeded in bringing down one of their craft, as detailed in a secret US government document quoted in Stanton Friedman's *Top Secret/Majic*, 'One of the crashes was the result of direct military action.'

My thesis is simple. Apart from reaffirming the veracity of

the existence of extraterrestrial visitors, my contention is that if we want to treat with them, we will need to do so via a different medium from those which we currently regard as normal. Fortunately, in accessing the spirit or ethereal part of our being, many previously unthinkable and 'paranormal' activities become possible. The convention of time ceases to be a constraint. Channelling, whereby people are able to receive communications from intelligent extraterrestrial entities, becomes possible. So does remote viewing, where the viewer is able to visit different points in the space–time continuum in spirit.

Lyssa Royal and Keith Priest make the point in their book *Preparing for Contact: A Metamorphosis of Consciousness* that, when Magellan circumnavigated the world, the natives of Patagonia could not 'see' his tall-masted ship because it was so far removed from their idea of reality. They interpreted what they saw according to the only guidelines they had – their own little boats. In the same way ancient literature refers to dragons and angels, which could well have been the only reference points for their sightings and experiences of extraterrestrials at that time.

In the same way, we have only occasional sightings of extraterrestrial spacecraft, and when people are abducted, no craft is generally in evidence. Is it that they are there and we are just unable to see them, in the same way that certain aircraft are 'invisible' to radar? Or are we simply not able to enter the dimensions inhabited by these craft? Had we mastered the ability to see in other dimensions, would these craft suddenly become visible to us? It seems that until we develop this faculty, we are limited to occasional sightings. And until such time as we are able to master other dimensions, the extraterrestrials studying our planet are able to abduct people at will.

So currently they are superior to us. They beat us in their power of thought control, and they are cleverer in being able to communicate by thought transference. We are primitive by comparison – both technologically and personally.

But we do have something that they want: we are genetically untainted. We represent great breeding potential for them – a harvest ground. They seem to be interested in us only for their breeding programme. They need to regenerate themselves and they will not disturb our culture while we supply them with what they require for that. They have no need to control us in a political sense if all they want is to milk humans for their reproductive genes.

EXTRATERRESTRIAL CONTACT

The aliens are smart enough to stay out of range and operate covertly. They once tried more open contact and did not succeed. We are too violent and reactive for them to do business on our terms.

As we shall see, when extraterrestrials abduct humans, they make them forget their experience. This is very significant. We do not go out of our way to upset wild animals, and just as we would study dangerous animals while keeping our distance, so they study us with the minimum of direct contact. They even appear to have persuaded some veteran abductees to act as minders to calm other more volatile abductees. Michelle LaVigne refers to them as 'empaths' in *The Alien Abduction Survival Guide*. It is possible that, as an extension of calming human fears about their activities, extraterrestrials are sending signals to channellers about their benevolent intentions. Perhaps the role of the channellers is to be recipients of psychological warfare (psych-ops) messages lulling mankind into a false sense of security.

So what should our attitude to them be? We should acknowledge the reality, study the situation and keep people from over-reacting and falling into despair. We also need to start being smarter, studying their technology and evolving to their level as rapidly as possible.

What do we know about them to date? At least we know what their spacecraft look like. In *Top Secret/Majic*, Stanton Friedman quotes the US government's *MJ-12 Special Operations Manual* which describes them as follows:

Documented extraterrestrial craft (UFOBs) are classified in one of four categories based on general shape, as follows:

a. Elliptical or disc shape. This type of craft is of a metallic construction and dull aluminum in color. They have the appearance of two pie-pans or shallow dishes pressed together and may have a raised dome on the top or bottom. No seams or joints are visible on the surface, giving the impression of one-piece construction. Discs are estimated from 50–300 feet in diameter and the thickness is approximately 15 percent of the diameter, not including the dome, which is 30 percent of the disc diameter and extends another 4–6 feet above the main body of the disc. The dome may or may not include windows or ports, and ports are present around the lower rim of the disk in some instances. Most disc-shaped craft are equipped with lights on the top and bottom, and also around the rim. These lights are not visible when the craft is at rest or not functioning. There are generally no visible antennae or projections. Landing gear consists of three extendible legs ending in circular landing pads. When fully extended this landing gear supports the mainbody 2–3 feet above the surface at the lowest point. A rectangular hatch is located along the equator or on the lower surface of the disc.

b. Fuselage or cigar shape. Documented reports of this type of craft are extremely rare. Air Force radar reports indicate they are approximately 2,000 feet long and 95 feet thick, and apparently they do not operate in the lower atmosphere. Very little information is available on the performance of these craft, but radar reports have indicated speeds in excess of 7,000 miles per hour. They do not appear to engage in the violent and erratic maneuvers associated with the smaller types.

c. Ovoid or circular shape. This type of craft is described as being shaped like an ice cream cone, being rounded at the large end and tapering to a near point at the other end. They are approximately 30–40 feet long and the thick end diameter is approximately 20 percent of the length. There is an extremely bright light at the pointed end, and this craft usually travels point down. They can appear to be any shape from round to cylindrical, depending upon the angle of observation. Often sightings of this type of craft are elliptical craft seen at an inclined angle or edge-on.

d. *Airfoil or triangular shape.* This craft is believed to be new technology due to the rarity and recency of the observations. Radar indicated an isosceles triangle profile, the longest side being nearly 300 feet in length. Little is known about the performance of these craft due to the rarity of good sightings, but they are believed capable of high speeds and abrupt maneuvers similar to or exceeding the performance attributed to types 'a' and 'c'.

We can assume that one of the craft described above is a description of the spacecraft that crashed outside Corona, near Roswell, New Mexico, in July 1947. Because the Roswell crash forms such an integral part of the UFO story, I shall review that next.

2

ROSWELL REVIEWED

Modern ufology traces its roots back to Roswell, New Mexico, where on the night of 2 July 1947, during a violent thunderstorm, a strange craft fell out of the sky. Many people in the area heard a loud crash that night, above the sound of the storm. The violence of the storms in this part of New Mexico is difficult to imagine until one has a direct experience of them. There have been many views about the nature of this craft. The US government would have us believe that the debris came from a weather balloon. Although the crash has become known as the Roswell Incident, the crash site is in fact nearer to Corona.

MAC BRAZEL'S FIND

The morning after the storm Mac Brazel, who worked as foreman on the Foster Ranch, found pieces of wreckage spread out over a large area of the ranch – more than half a mile long. When he drove back home he showed a piece of the wreckage to his neighbours, Floyd and Loretta Proctor. The material was unlike anything they had ever seen before.

A few days later, on 6 July, he drove into Roswell where he showed pieces of the wreckage to George Wilcox, Chaves County Sheriff. Wilcox immediately called the local military airfield, Roswell Army Air Field (RAAF) – the US Air Force was still an operational arm of the army at that time. He spoke by phone to Major Jesse Marcel, intelligence officer of the 509th Bomb Group, which was stationed at the airfield.

The 509th Bomb Group is no ordinary unit. It is one of the most famous units in the US Air Force. It was formed in 1944 as the 509th Composite Group for one specific task – to deliver the atomic bomb to Japan in the Second World War. And the runway at Roswell AAF is no ordinary runway. At that time, despite its remote location, it was the longest in the USA. It was also home in 1945 and 1946 to 'Enola Gay', the B-29 bomber from which the atomic bomb was dropped on Hiroshima.

Marcel drove to Wilcox's office and inspected the wreckage. He reported to his commanding officer, Colonel William 'Butch' Blanchard, who had narrowly missed being chosen to fly the aeroplane from which the first atomic bomb was dropped. He ordered Marcel to take someone from the counter-intelligence section and inspect the crash site, and to bring back as much of the wreckage material as he could.

Marcel and Sheridan Cavitt of the Counter-intelligence Corps drove to the ranch with Mac Brazel, arriving late in the evening of 6 July. They spent the night in an outbuilding on the ranch and inspected the crash site the following morning. At the same time, military police from the airfield arrived at the Sheriff Wilcox's office, where they collected pieces of wreckage and returned to the airfield.

While the two military men were on their way to Mac Brazel's ranch, the story swept through the desert town like wildfire. Someone telephoned radio station KSWS in Albuquerque where Lydia Sleppy began transmitting the news on the teletype. As she was typing the story, her transmission was interrupted by the bell signalling an incoming call on the wire. The message read, 'This is the FBI. You will cease transmitting.'

Marcel and Cavitt collected pieces of wreckage from the crash site. Cavitt left the site and returned the next day to Roswell AAF with as much material as he could fit into his vehicle. Marcel continued collecting wreckage at the site and drove home where he spent the night, before reporting to his commanding officer the next morning.

Jesse Marcel Jr recalls the evening that his father returned with pieces of debris from what appeared to be a crashed spacecraft. He was 11 years old at the time, but he recalls the event clearly, for it made an indelible impression upon him. He went on to become a medical doctor, a National Guard helicopter pilot and flight surgeon, a Vietnam veteran, and a qualified accident investigator. He can therefore be regarded as a credible witness, despite his youth at the time of the crash. He recalls how his father woke both him and his mother at around two o'clock in the morning and showed them some pieces of an unusual material which he spread out so that they could get a better view. They all came to the conclusion that the material was not of earthly origin. He remembers that the debris had strange pink and purple symbols embossed on the inside of some of the metal 'I-beam' pieces. The symbols reminded him of ancient Egyptian hieroglyphics, except that they did not include any of the animal symbols usually found in Egyptian inscriptions.

The next morning, on July 8, both Marcel and Cavitt arrived back at Roswell AAF with their carloads of debris. Colonel Blanchard immediately had the wreckage flown to the head-quarters of the Eighth Air Force, of which the 509th Bomb Group was part, in Fort Worth, Texas. It was subsequently flown to Air Force headquarters in Washington for further inspection. Major Marcel was ordered to accompany the wreckage to Fort Worth.

The military's press release

Later that day, Colonel Blanchard instructed Second Lieutenant Walter Haut, the Public Information Officer for the 509th Bomb Group, to issue a press release revealing the story of his unit's discovery of the remnants of a crashed alien spacecraft. Haut drove to KGFL, Roswell's radio station, where he gave the press release to Frank Joyce, a station employee. Joyce recalls the onion-skin paper on which the press release was typed. He phoned Haut from the radio station after the latter had returned to the airfield to confirm the story before sending it on to the United Press bureau, and suggested that Haut should reconsider the decision to release a story that claimed that his unit had discovered a 'flying saucer or flying disk'. Haut assured him that the press release had been approved by Colonel Blanchard. The text of the press release reads as follows:

> The many rumors regarding the flying disc became a reality yesterday when the intelligence office of the 509th Bomb Group of the Eighth Air Force, Roswell Army Air Field, was fortunate enough to gain possession of a disc through the cooperation of one of the local ranchers and the sheriff's office of Chaves County.
>
> The flying object landed on a ranch near Roswell sometime last week. Not having phone facilities, the rancher stored the disk until such time as he was able to contact the sheriff's office, who in turn notified Major Jesse A Marcel of the 509th Bomb Group Intelligence Office.
>
> Action was immediately taken and the disc was picked up at the rancher's home. It was inspected at Roswell Army Air Field and subsequently loaned by Major Marcel to higher headquarters.

Calls came flooding into the radio station on the teletype in response to the story, but then suddenly the line went dead – it just hummed. Shortly afterwards the station received a threatening call from someone who claimed to be calling from the Pentagon. Joyce told the mysterious caller that his information was based on a press release from the US Army Air Corps. The caller slammed the phone down.

After many years of silence on the subject, in an interview in 1992 with *Air and Space* magazine, Haut tersely revealed his own view of the events in Roswell in 1947: 'I feel that there was a crash of an extraterrestrial vehicle near Corona.'

Frank Joyce kept his copy of the press release that Walter Haut had given him, as proof that he had not invented the story. Walt Whitmore, owner of the radio station, telephoned him in a state of considerable agitation. It seemed that someone had already warned him off the story. Frank Joyce later gave the document to Whitmore, and that was the last that he saw of it.

The local newspaper, the *Roswell Daily Record* had already picked up the story. Its midday edition on 8 July, carried a front-page article and a blazing headline: 'RAAF Captures Flying Saucer on Ranch in Roswell Region'.

The weather balloon story

That same afternoon, on 8 July 1947, General Clemence McMullen in Washington spoke on the telephone to Colonel Thomas DuBose, Chief of Staff to General Roger Ramey, Commander of the Eighth Air Force. McMullen ordered General Ramey to quash the flying saucer story by creating a cover story. He also ordered DuBose to have pieces of the wreckage flown to Washington.

Later in the afternoon, General Ramey held a press conference at the headquarters of the Eighth Air Force in Fort Worth. He announced that what had crashed at Corona was not a flying saucer. Colonel Blanchard and his officers had misidentified a weather balloon with a radar reflector. Could such a simple mistake be made by a man who was a candidate for the mission that ended the war in the Pacific, a man described by those who knew him as a 'no-nonsense', businesslike individual, unlikely to make elementary errors, a man who went on to become a four-star general and Vice Chief of Staff of the US Air Force?

To add credibility to this cover story, Major Jesse Marcel was brought in to show the press pieces of an actual weather balloon. The real debris had by this time disappeared into the maw of the military, never to be seen again. Although many of the newspapers in the West and Midwest had already carried the original flying saucer story, the morning editions of the *New York Times*, the *Washington Post*, and the *Chicago Tribune* obligingly carried the cover-up story the next day.

THE SECOND FIND

Meanwhile, back in New Mexico, a large group of soldiers was sent to the Foster Ranch to collect all traces of wreckage. They scoured the surrounding countryside for debris while military police sealed off the area. Even Sheriff George Wilcox was stopped at the security perimeter. After a day or two a second crash site was discovered about 2 miles away. Here the main body of the spacecraft was found, with the bodies of four small humanoid creatures.

Mac Brazel was taken into custody by the military. After a few days he was seen in Roswell with military personnel who accompanied him as an escort guard. He declined to speak to any of his friends while he was accompanied. After his release, he repudiated his original story of having found the wreckage of something unearthly. Marian Strickland, one of his neighbours, formed the impression that he had been threatened against talking openly about the incident. Barbara Dugger, George Wilcox's granddaughter, confirmed that the military had made threats to her grandfather, the local sheriff to whom Mac Brazel had originally brought the pieces of debris. Her grandmother had urged her not to talk to anyone about the incident. She revealed that the military police came to the sheriff's office at the jailhouse and threatened to have him and his whole family killed if they talked about what had taken place.

And so began the policy of the United States government – of deceit, public denial, cover-up and death threats – with regard to the subject of extraterrestrial encounters.

The testimony of Glenn Dennis, the Roswell mortician

While visiting Roswell in the summer of 1996 I met Glenn Dennis, who is President of the Roswell International UFO Museum and Research Center. I found him to be a polite, straightforward and credible person. He did not strike me as someone who wanted to capitalize on his story. Indeed, he had lived in complete anonymity for more than 40 years, away from the glare of UFO publicity, until he was 'discovered' by Stanton Friedman. He seemed slightly uncomfortable with the amount of media attention to which he was regularly subjected.

He has given many interviews over the years about his involvement with the strange events at Roswell in July 1947. He reveals how at junior high school in Roswell, when the class was being asked what they wanted to do for a living, he blurted out that he wanted to be an undertaker in order to get a laugh from the class. But when he was asked to write a report on the subject, his fascination developed.

In 1947 Glenn Dennis was working for Ballard Funeral Homes where he was in charge of the company's military contract work, providing ambulance and mortuary services to the forces. He received a call from the mortuary officer at the Roswell AAF during the afternoon of 9 July. He asked Dennis if he had any baby caskets, or small hermetically sealed ones, about 3 feet 6 inches or 4 feet long. Dennis told him that he always kept a 4-foot casket in stock. It had a metal inner liner with a rubber gasket, and could be sealed airtight. The mortuary officer asked how many there were in stock, and Dennis said he had two. There were also standard-sized caskets of 3 feet 6 inches, but these would have to be ordered from the supplier in Amarillo, Texas. Provided he phoned them before three o'clock, they would be delivered by six o'clock the next morning.

After about 30 minutes the mortuary officer called again and asked various questions about the preparation of bodies. He asked about embalming fluids and their chemical compounds. He asked about treating bodies that had been lying in the open. He wanted to know how bodies that had been shredded by predators and exposed to the elements for a week to ten days should be treated. He asked specifically about alterations to the blood, stomach contents and skin tissue. Dennis told him about tests for poison and how the blood would be affected. When he asked what the mortuary officer was dealing with, he was told that the information was for future use. Dennis offered his assistance if it was needed.

Shortly afterwards the officer called a third time and asked Dennis about the removal of a body that had been lying out in the New Mexico sun at a daytime temperature of around 110 degrees for a week or more. Dennis told him that after such exposure, a body is likely to fall apart when lifted: 'When you pick up a hand, you're going to have just the hand.' He told the officer to use dry ice from Clardy's Dairy or Sunset Creamery in which to pack the bodies. He also advised the mortuary office to use a pathologist if there was uncertainty about the cause of death; Dennis recommended the Walter

Reed Army Hospital in Washington. He again offered his services in the preparation of the bodies.

About 45 minutes later, Dennis received a call for the ambulance service to attend an airman who had been injured in a crash on his motorcycle. He had a laceration on the forehead and a broken nose. Dennis provided some roadside first aid, then seated the airman on the front seat of the hearse/ ambulance and drove him back to the airfield. He turned on the red light as usual when he approached the front gate, so that he was waved through without stopping. He drove to the infirmary, where three military field ambulances were at the ramp where Dennis usually parked his vehicle when making deliveries or collections. He therefore parked to the side and walked up the ramp with the injured airman, approaching the field ambulances from the rear.

Two military policemen were standing beside the ambulances, two of which had their rear doors open. As a matter of professional curiosity, Dennis glanced inside the first vehicle as he approached. He saw some debris. One piece looked like the broken half of a canoe standing on its end, between 3 and 4 feet high. The others looked sharp and jagged, like broken glass. Some of the pieces, including the 'canoe', looked like stainless steel that had been exposed to high temperatures, shaded in a gradation of colour from high gloss, to pink, to red, to brown and then black. Having worked on crashed military aircraft at nearby Fort Sumner, when the mortuary had a contract with them, Dennis was aware of the blue-purple hue of stainless steel that had been exposed to extreme temperatures. Along the outer edge of the canoe-shaped object were markings, just over an inch high, that looked to Dennis like ancient Egyptian hieroglyphics. The second ambulance contained similar debris. The injured airman also saw the material in the ambulances, but was understandably more concerned with his injuries than with the ambulances and their contents.

One of the military policemen walked with Dennis and the airman to the check-in desk inside the infirmary where Dennis collected the voucher that ensured payment for his services. He did not take in the airman's name. He then made his way to the doctors' and nurses' lounge area, as he usually did when visiting the airbase, to get a Coke and to see what was going on. There was more activity and commotion than usual, and a number of high-ranking officers whom Dennis did not recognize, despite his familiarity with all the medical officers working at the base.

As he walked further down the hallway, Dennis saw a captain whom he did not know, leaning against a doorway talking to someone inside. He said to him, 'Looks like you've had a crash. Do I need to get ready for it?'

The captain looked at him and said, 'Who the hell are you?'

Dennis told him that he was from the funeral home in Roswell that had the contract to provide mortuary services to Roswell AAF, and that pieces of wreckage were usually brought to the mortuary garage, where the identifications were made and bodies and wreckage untangled and reassembled. The captain said, 'You wait right here. Don't take a step. Wait right here.' He returned with two military policemen and told them to remove Dennis from the base and to drive him back to town.

They had walked only a few paces when a voice called out, 'Bring that son of a bitch back.' As they turned, Dennis was approached by a tall captain with crew-cut red hair, accompanied by a sergeant carrying a clipboard. The captain said forcefully, 'Look mister, you don't go into Roswell and start rumours that there's been a crash. There's no crash. There never was a crash. Nothing has happened here. You understand?' As the captain spoke he poked a finger in Dennis' chest. Dennis became angry at the officer's manner and replied, 'I'm a civilian and you can't do anything to me. So as far as I'm concerned, you can go to hell.' The red-haired captain came back with, 'Let me tell you, mister, somebody will be picking your bones out of the sand.' The sergeant chimed in with, 'Sir, he'd make better dog food.' The captain turned to the military policemen and said, 'Get this son of a bitch out of here.'

As they walked down the hallway, an army nurse with whom Glenn Dennis was on friendly terms came running into the hallway with a towel over her mouth. She screamed and told

Dennis to get out of the infirmary as fast as he could; that he was going to be in a lot of trouble if he did not. She was sobbing and gasping for air as she continued across the hallway followed by two men wearing surgeon's jackets. They were also gasping for air and looked as if they were about to vomit. Dennis did not himself smell or see anything strange. One of the MPs escorting him seemed puzzled by the brief exchange. They then drove behind Dennis, following him to the funeral home, and advised him to stay away from the base for the remainder of the day.

Later that evening, Dennis phoned the infirmary and the nurses' home, trying to reach his friend without success. She was from a devout Catholic family in St Paul, Minnesota, and had recently graduated from nursing school. She had been commissioned only three months previously, and Roswell AAF was her first assignment. Dennis tried to reach her again the next morning, again without success. Then at around eleven o'clock she rang and said that she knew that Dennis had been trying to reach her, but that she had been sick. She said that she could not talk on the phone, but would meet Dennis for lunch if he wanted to know more. He suggested the officers' club which was near the nurses' home and where his company had corporate membership.

The alien autopsy

Dennis drove directly to the club, where his friend was already waiting outside for him. The club was relatively empty and they sat at a table at the back. She looked dishevelled and seemed to be in a state of shock. She made Dennis promise never to repeat the story she was about to tell him; otherwise she would be in a lot of trouble. She asked him if he had brought the 'creatures' to the funeral home; but he told her that he had not seen any bodies. The nurse then took a prescription pad from one of her pockets and made some drawings, after extracting a further solemn oath from Dennis that he would never reveal her connection with the drawings or the 'creatures'. She asked him to guard the drawings with his life. She described her experience of the previous day as the most horrible and gruesome in her life.

She explained that, unlike her colleagues, she had not received instructions that the infirmary staff were not to report for duty that day. She had therefore gone to the supplies room as usual at the beginning of her shift. There she saw two doctors in surgical garb and masks, standing over one of two wheeled stretchers. On each was an unzipped body bag. The body bag over which the doctors were leaning contained two small, mangled bodies. The abdomens and legs were crushed, and appeared to have been partially eaten by predators. The third body looked intact. The smell, she said, was the vilest she had ever experienced. She was about to leave the room when the two doctors stopped her. Although she said she was busy, they demanded that she stay and write on a pad as they dictated. So she stayed and wrote down their commentary of the autopsy.

A hand from one of the bodies was severed from the arm. When they turned the hand over using a long forceps, they saw that it had four fingers and no thumb, and instead of fingernails, it had little suction cups or pads at the end of each finger. The heads were disproportionately large and flexible, like those of newborn babies, and had no hair. Their eyes were large and sunk deep into their sockets; they could not be seen clearly. Their mouths were just slits about an inch wide. They had no teeth, just a piece of tissue, like cartilage. The noses were concave, with no bridge and two small orifices. The ears had two canals, unlike those of humans, which have only one, and no earlobes, although the doctors described two flaps which closed over both aural canals. There were no visible sexual organs. Finally she reported that the bone from the shoulder to the elbow was much shorter than the one from the elbow to the wrist; and that the doctors from time to time checked the intact body to compare it with the body they were examining, which was between $3\frac{1}{2}$ and 4 feet tall.

Eventually all three of them were overwhelmed by the smell and began to feel sick. The doctors were concerned that the air-conditioning ducts might carry the smell through the hospital. They decided to stop, and remove the bodies elsewhere for further examination, whereupon they dismissed the nurse. She left the examining room with a towel over her mouth, and it was then that she encountered Dennis being escorted from the infirmary. She returned to the nurses' quarters, where the other nurses found the smell so offensive that they helped her shower and wash her hair in an attempt to get rid of it.

When Dennis asked her about the doctors, she said that she had never seen either of them before, but that one of them had said something about finishing up this work and returning to Walter Reed Army Hospital in Washington, DC. According to the head nurse, Captain Wilson, the bodies were moved to a hangar where the autopsies were completed that night, and were then flown to Wright Field (now Wright-Patterson Air Force Base) at Dayton, Ohio. Dennis's friend had also heard that the bodies were found near the wreckage, about 2 or 3 miles from the site where the debris was initially found.

She was still in a state of shock, and Dennis drove her back to the nurses' quarters in silence.

The nurse's disappearance

That was the last time Glenn Dennis saw his friend. When he asked about her a few days later at the base, he was told that she had been posted elsewhere. Six weeks later he received a typed letter addressed to the Ballard Funeral Home, without his name in the address, and a note from her with a New York APO number (an address code for US forces overseas). She wrote that she was now in London, and wanted to know what had happened to him. He immediately replied that he was still curious and would like to know more. Two months later his letter was returned with the words 'Return to Sender' across the front of the envelope and the word 'Deceased' stamped in red at the bottom.

Dennis later mentioned the returned letter to Captain Wilson and asked if she knew what happened to his friend. She said she had heard that the nurse had been in a plane that crashed on a training mission. Many researchers have attempted to identify the accident and locate the nurse, without success.

Dennis stored her drawings in an old filing cabinet at the Ballard Funeral Home, and left them behind with various personal and legal papers when he left in 1962. He returned some years later with UFO researcher Stanton Friedman, but they found that the filing cabinets had been emptied, and the contents thrown onto the town dump in a general clearout.

UFO investigators trying to identify Dennis' friend found the files missing of all five nurses pictured in the 1947 Roswell Army Air Field Yearbook. Philip Klass, a renowned UFO sceptic, subsequently revealed that the nurse's name was Naomi Maria Selff; but Glenn Dennis refused to confirm or deny his claim. Dennis has also been criticized by sceptical reporters because the information provided by him has varied in minor details between one interview and another. Dennis points out, however, that he only began to recall his experience of the strange events in Roswell more then thirty years later, when he was first interviewed by Stanton Friedman. Given his general nervousness when being interviewed, and the length of time that has passed, it is understandable, he says, that he may have sometimes become confused on small items of detail, but he asserts that the basic facts of the story are as he has related them.

THE NATURE OF THE DEBRIS

Jesse Marcel's description

In an interview in 1979 Jesse Marcel revealed his role in the Roswell story. He talked about arriving at the Foster Ranch with Sheridan Cavitt, although Cavitt to this day denies both the event and any knowledge of the Foster Ranch. Marcel describes the area as having being strewn with fragments over an area about three-quarters of a mile long and several hundred feet wide. To Marcel, the debris looked as though it had come from an object travelling very fast that had exploded above the ground. Although they loaded as much as they could into a jeep which Cavitt drove back to the base, that was only a small proportion of the crash fragments. Marcel continued to collect debris which he loaded into his car.

As he and Cavitt collected the wreckage, Marcel noticed that some of the material was very light yet would not bend. While it was like parchment, no thicker than the foil paper used in packets of cigarettes, the material could not be dented, bent or burned. Not even a 16-pound sledgehammer could make an impression. Marcel was familiar with airborne objects of all kinds and it was evident that this was not part of an aeroplane, a missile or a weather balloon.

So he knew the weather balloon story was untrue and, as his son revealed subsequently, he was disturbed by his obligation to hide the truth, but his security classification depended on him doing so. However, he was no 'fall-guy'. By maintaining his security rating, he was able to go on to perform a number of important assignments, the most noteworthy of which was the compilation of a report on the first Soviet nuclear detonation, which went directly to the desk of the President of the United States.

The civilians' descriptions

Loretta Proctor, one of Mac Brazel's nearest neighbours, described some of the material that he brought for them to look at. One piece was about 4 inches long, tan-coloured and as light as balsa wood, but without any visible grain. It felt smooth like plastic; but they were unable to cut it with a knife or to burn it.

Bessie Brazel Schreiber, Mac Brazel's daughter, described some of the wreckage from the crash as being like aluminium foil, with incomprehensible symbols in columns. Another piece was of the same material but shaped like a pipe, about 4 inches in diameter and 4 inches long, and flanged at one end.

William Brazel Jr, Mac Brazel's son, described other pieces of the wreckage as like tin foil that returned to its original shape after being wrinkled, creased or folded. The material could not be torn or broken. When it unfolded itself and reverted to its original flat shape, it left no crease or indication that it had been folded. He noticed this characteristic when he folded a piece in order to store it in a cigar box.

He also described some pieces of the wreckage as being as light as balsa wood, with a more neutral tan colour, but flexible and pliable. The material contained no visible grain and proved impossible to cut or break; or even to score with a pocket knife. Although this particular material contained no writing or markings, there were other pieces with markings which reminded him of the petrographs or figurines which had been drawn on rocks by the local native Americans.

According to William Brazel Jr, his father had been asked by the Air Force to take an oath not to discuss in any detail his findings at the crash site. Mac Brazel was an old-style cowboy for whom an oath was not something to be taken lightly, and he hardly ever spoke about the incident or the material again. While at a pool hall in Corona about a month after the crash, however, his son talked openly about the fragments of the strange material that he had collected. A day or two later an officer named Armstrong with a sergeant and two other soldiers turned up at the ranch. They asked for the fragments, reminded him of the oath that his father had taken and cautioned him against speaking about the incident or the material.

Dr Lincoln La Paz's investigation

An officer in the Counter-intelligence Corps, Bill Rickett, who was based at Roswell, was asked shortly after the crash to escort a meteor expert around the crash site. The expert was Dr Lincoln La Paz, head of the Department of Mathematics and Astronomy at the University of New Mexico, and was also the Director of the Institute of Meteoritics, which was formed in 1944 as the first institute in the world to be devoted exclusively to the research of meteorites and planetary samples. Dr La Paz was an acknowledged expert on trajectories of meteors and meteorites. His brief was to determine the speed and trajectory of the alien craft. Initially they examined some of the wreckage recovered from the Foster Ranch, and they found the material to be very strong and very light. It was flexible, but they could neither break it nor put a crease or mark on it.

Dr La Paz seemed particularly interested in Mac Brazel's information that some of his animals had behaved strangely after the crash. When he was flown over the area, he determined from marks on the ground that the object has touched down a few miles from the initial crash site, and then taken off again. The sand at the spot where the craft had touched down had been turned into a glass-like substance, and they collected samples. They also found more of the thin foil-like material. Dr La Paz told Bill Rickett that he thought the craft had touched down for repairs and taken off again before exploding. He felt sure that it was one of many similar craft and that the accident was due to system malfunction.

Despite his learning, Dr La Paz had an easy manner with people, and was also able to speak to many of the local ranch hands in Spanish. Some of them had noticed strange craft flying over the area very slowly, at a low altitude, two days after the crash. Dr La Paz felt certain that they had been searching for their downed craft. The local people also noticed that their animals had been affected.

Rickett and La Paz agreed that the Air Force's story of a weather balloon was untrue, but although they speculated on the possibility of a higher civilization checking on the Earth, Dr La Paz decided to leave any speculation out of his report.

The craft had gouged a furrow in Mac Brazel's field about 500 feet long and 10 feet wide, but it was not clear which part of the craft had done the damage. The power source was never found and the main body of the craft, which contained the bodies, was found some 2 miles away. It seems likely therefore that the power source and the main body had become forcibly separated, through either system failure or a lightning strike. And although the materials found were extraordinarily light, the furrow must have been made by a very heavy component – possibly the power source before it exploded, spreading its debris across Mac Brazel's field.

The military witnesses

Despite what many Hollywood films would have us believe, most military operations, however small, involve a supporting cast of hundreds, even thousands, of minor, and usually unnoticed, players. Their role may be small in relation to the whole, but it can be crucial in reconstructing the event. The testimony of each individual contributes to demonstrate the undeniable actuality of the event. In the late 1980s, therefore, nuclear physicist and UFO researcher Stanton Friedman led the search to unearth some of the military people involved in the recovery and movement of the extraterrestrial detritus from the crash site to Roswell AAF, and on to Fort Worth AAF, in 1947.

Master Sergeant Robert Porter, brother of Mac Brazel's neighbour Loretta Proctor, was flight engineer on the first B-29 which flew the special cargo to Eighth Air Force headquarters at Fort Worth AAF, Texas, in 1947. He remembers that the deputy commander of the 509th Bomb Group, Lieutenant Colonel Payne Jennings, was on board with Major Jesse Marcel. One of the flight crew, Captain Anderson, said that the cargo was from a flying saucer. He recalls the extraordinarily light weight of some of the packages, as if they were empty.

After landing at Fort Worth, while the engineering crew performed routine maintenance checks on the plane and ate lunch, the packages were transferred to a B-25 that flew them to Wright Field at Dayton, Ohio. Master Sergeant Porter and the crew were told that the cargo was from a weather balloon – a story that they all knew had been concocted.

Staff Sergeant Robert Shuster was on the second flight to Fort Worth AAF, which carried the alien corpses. He recalls four armed military policemen on the flight (an unusual precaution for a weather balloon), guarding a specially made crate that was 12 feet long by 5 feet wide and 4 feet high.

The flight was also unusual in that the plane was flown at a low altitude between 4,000 and 5,000 feet, and the cabin was unpressurized – possibly an added safety precaution for an unusually precious cargo. The return flight was at the usual altitude of 25,000 feet, with the cabin pressurized. While it was rumoured that the aircraft was carrying debris from the unusual crash, Robert Shuster was not himself aware of any bodies being transported.

Robert Smith was a member of the First Air Transport Unit, which was also based at Roswell AAF in 1947. He was part of the team that loaded crates of debris onto transport planes. During the operation, one of the team came across a fragment, between 2 and 3 inches square. The unusual material had jagged edges and could not be permanently folded or creased. Even when it was crumpled, it unfolded itself to its former shape, making a crackling noise as it did so, like cellophane. Despite the armed guard, Smith's colleague, a sergeant, was able to put the strange fragment into his pocket.

Most of the crates, which were loaded onto three or four cargo planes, were 2 or 3 feet high by 2 feet square. Smith recalls however that one was much larger than the others. It was about 20 feet long by 4 or 5 feet wide and 4 or 5 feet high. He recognized 'Pappy' Henderson's flight crew around the plane on to which the crates were loaded – Captain Oliver Wendell Henderson, known as 'Pappy' in the Air Force. The loading operation was supervised by a number of people in plain clothes who flashed a strange ID when challenged and said that they were from a project whose name Smith could not recall. The loading crew was told that the crates were from a crashed plane, although crashed planes were usually taken to the salvage yard and not flown out in crates under armed guard.

'Pappy' Henderson was a highly respected Second World War bomber pilot who was based at Roswell AAF after the war. He was one of the very few pilots chosen to fly scientists and atomic materials from Roswell (which was close to Los Alamos) to the Pacific for atomic weapons testing. His work required a top-secret clearance and a level of discretion that he applied to all his work. In 1980–1981, while living in San Diego, he read a newspaper article about a UFO and alien bodies having been discovered outside Roswell in 1947. He showed it to his wife, Sappho, and asked her to read it. He confirmed that the story was true, and that he was the pilot who flew the wreckage of the UFO to Wright Field, Dayton, Ohio. He told her that he had wanted to tell her about it for years, and now felt that he could, since it was in the newspaper. He described the bodies that were being transported as being much smaller than humans, with large heads and eyes that were sunken and slanted. They wore clothing that was unlike anything he had ever seen before.

Further evidence that the material was taken to Wright Field is provided by Lieutenant Colonel Arthur E Exon, who was stationed there in July 1947. Exon, who went on to retire with the rank of General, confirmed in 1990 that the Roswell wreckage was brought into their material laboratories, and that some of it was very thin but very strong and could not be dented with heavy hammers. He went on to state that the overall consensus was that the pieces were from space.

Sergeant Melvin Brown was a cook at Roswell AAF in 1947. He remembers that all available men were hurriedly taken out to guard a disc that had crashed outside Roswell. They later stood guard outside some hangars at the airfield itself. He travelled from the crash site back to Roswell AAF in the back of one of the trucks with another soldier. He was puzzled that some of the trucks were packed with dry ice.

They were ordered not to look under the covering, but it would be a most unusual person who could resist taking a peek, regardless of orders. What they saw utterly astonished them. Brown described the two dead alien bodies as smaller than normal men. They were about 4 feet tall with larger heads than ours and slanted eyes. Their bodies were yellow and Asian-looking according to Brown. When asked if he was scared, Brown described the alien bodies as looking 'nice, almost as though they would be friendly if they were alive'.

THE WEATHER BALLOON STORY CONTINUES

In view of the diverse and extensive testimony to the effect that the crash was of an alien spacecraft, it seems extraordinary that the US government and military still maintain the fiction that it was a weather balloon. It is somewhat perverse to bring in an expert on meteorites to inspect a weather balloon and to calculate its trajectory. Moreover, according to Jesse Marcel, a weather balloon would not have generated sufficient debris to cover such a vast area; and he would immediately have recognized the fragments brought into Sheriff Wilcox's office by Mac Brazel had they been from a weather balloon. It also seems highly unlikely that Colonel 'Butch' Blanchard, who went on to become a four-star general, would have made such a basic mistake. The weather officer at the airfield would immediately have identified a weather balloon and brought this strange episode to an abrupt end.

Certainly, the components of a weather balloon would not have had the unusual characteristics of the material that Jesse Marcel and Sheridan Cavitt collected from the Foster Ranch. And it is bizarre for a government to impose such strict security over a weather balloon.

Why, one wonders, does the US government still maintain such a strict shroud of secrecy, 50 years after the event while fabricating a number of constantly changing cover stories. In 1994 the US government issued a 23-page report stating that what crashed was not a weather balloon, but a highly secret balloon, used to detect Russian atomic tests. Then, in June 1997, the US government issued another report which acknowledged for the first time that there were bodies found in the wreckage of the Roswell Incident. This report, called 'Case Closed' claimed that the bodies were 'probably' test dummies used to test parachutes.

This new version of the government's story is called into question by information that dummies were not used for crash testing until 1953, six years after the crash near Roswell. As one of the visitors to the 50th anniversary held in Roswell in July 1997 observed, 'You have to be a real dummy to believe the dummy story.'

3

SIGHTINGS

The purpose of this chapter is to establish the actuality of extraterrestrial visitors in the minds of those readers for whom reality is primarily determined by visual evidence.

The majority of unidentified flying objects cease to be 'unidentified' once they are investigated. Many are shown to have been lights, swamp gas or various other natural phenomena. There remain however a hard core of about 10 per cent of sightings for which no natural explanation is found. The evidence to explain these cases often disappears into government archives. The military teams which perform the investigations have been known to report only the explainable cases in the government files which then later become available to public scrutiny. The truly mysterious cases are removed at an early stage to another investigation category.

TYPES OF ENCOUNTER

In order to overcome government obstruction many private organizations have sprung up to investigate UFO phenomena themselves (*see* Appendix: UFO Organizations).

One of the most readable and comprehensive books on the subject is *Uninvited Guests: A Documented History of UFO Sightings, Alien Encounters and Coverup* by Richard Hall, former Assistant Director of the National Investigations Committee on Aerial Phenomena (NICAP). The author provides a representative sample of 53 encounters in 19 countries, which he categorizes by their effects: electromagnetic, levitation of the subject, sound, steering loss, psychological effects, brilliant light, heat, physical traces and abduction. From the viewpoint of the physical evidence, the electromagnetic effects which render motor vehicles inoperable while spacecraft are in the vicinity are most convincing. As Hall notes, 'Machines do not hallucinate.'

Encounters with extraterrestrials are referred to by Dr J Allen Hynek of the Center for UFO Studies as close encounters (CE). He classifies them as close encounters of the first kind (CE1), the second kind (CE2), the third kind (CE3), etc. CE1 refers to observation of a UFO within 150 yards, while CE2 is a sighting of a UFO which leaves some physical evidence, such as a burn mark where it touched the ground. A close encounter of the third kind, CE3, is a visual sighting of an occupant or entity from a UFO, possibly with some interaction with them. An abduction would be classed as a CE4, while a CE5 would be some form of direct communication with an extraterrestrial being, through channelling or actual contact.

Richard and Lee Boylan, in *Close Extraterrestrial Encounters*, define a CE4 as 'a physical visit to the immediate location of a human being by one or more extraterrestrial, three-dimensional, intelligent beings (ETs), usually for the purposes of communication, education or removal to a UFO craft for specific procedures.'

Close encounters with unidentified flying objects, and claims of contact with alien beings, are among the most widely reported phenomena in the world today. Thousands of sightings and contacts are recorded each year. While less than 10 per cent are likely to remain unexplained, it is also likely that no more than 10 per cent of all encounters are actually reported. They occur in all parts of the world and often involve physical evidence such as photographs and radar tracks, electrical disruptions and marks on the ground as well as human physiological effects.

But the study of UFOs is hampered by the alleged government cover-up of known sightings and contacts. Without doubt, various agencies of the US government have taken more interest in UFOs than they have been willing to admit. Military encounters with UFOs, both in the USA and other countries, have shown that UFOs easily out-perform the most capable aircraft pitted against them. Furthermore, the UFOs are able to inflict lethal damage on human craft without risk of damage to themselves.

In the forefront of current UFO research is the so-called 'abduction' phenomenon, in which humans claim to have been taken by alien beings into unusual environments where quasi-medical operations are performed. Often these encounters have a gynaecological or reproductive focus. Some experiencers, abductees and researchers believe that abduction is aimed mainly at creating alien–human hybrid beings. Experiencers also say they are often told about world problems and given predictions, usually of disaster.

But alien encounters, even abductions, are not always unpleasant. Some abductees characterize their experiences as neutral. Most, however, seem not unnaturally to resent the powerlessness of their situation. Some report encounters with truly benign, even spiritually enthralling entities. Channellers such as Lyssa Royal and Barbara Hand Clow interpret extra-terrestrial contacts as truly life-enhancing – an opportunity to extend and project our lives beyond the realm of physical reality. Michelle LaVigne's *The Alien Abduction Survival Guide*, on the other hand, is the first of a genre of collaborators' guidebooks on how to retain a sense of self-respect, despite one's resentment at being made completely powerless. One abductee has made the observation, 'When you control your fear, the grey's immobilization technology doesn't seem to work as efficiently as before.' (Andrew Brough, *Soul Manipulation and Free-Will*.)

Such dichotomies arouse great controversy. One view is that there is a positive intention behind the abduction phenomenon and that negative emotions are caused by our misunderstanding – that the term 'abduction' is both misleading and pejorative.

Many abductees report telepathic communication with aliens. Some say that aliens can telepathically control human thought and behaviour. Others claim to be receiving important telepathic information from alien sources via channelling; an increasing number of books are devoted exclusively to information channelled from extraterrestrial sources.

The question of what is behind such experiences remains unresolved. If alien beings are involved, their origin and nature remains unknown. The 'extraterrestrial hypothesis' that UFOs are intelligently controlled by beings from other worlds, favoured by some UFO researchers, is regarded by many others as insufficient to account for the extreme strangeness of many reports.

Many astronomers and space scientists today agree that it is highly probable that there is other intelligent life in the galaxy, but most do not believe that even very advanced beings could traverse interstellar space to reach the earth. Hardcore sceptics dismiss claims of UFOs and aliens as nothing but products of human error, delusion or outright lies and hoaxes. But growing numbers of open-minded professionals concede that something really is going on.

TYPES OF ALIEN BEINGS

The alien beings that have been seen are often referred to as 'greys', but this is apparently only one type of being invading our airspace; they are from Zeta Reticuli, and appear to be here to replenish their genetic stock. Channellers, who receive communications from extraterrestrial worlds, have identified 14 different types of alien beings (see chapter 6). And by 1954 the US government had already identified two types which they described in a secret manual on the handling of contact with extraterrestrials (published in Stanton Friedman's *Top Secret/Majic*). They are called EBEs (extraterrestrial biological entities) in this secret US government document.

Examination of remains recovered from wreckage of UFOBs indicates that Extraterrestrial Biological Entities may be classified into two distinct categories as follows:

a. *EBE Type I.* These entities are humanoid and might be mistaken for human beings of the Oriental race if seen from a distance. They are bi-pedal, 5 feet to 5 feet 4 inches in height and weigh 80–100 pounds. Proportionately they are similar to humans, although the cranium is somewhat larger and more rounded. The skin is a pale, chalky-yellow in color, thick, and slightly pebbled in appearance. The eyes are small, wide-set, almond-shaped, with brownish-black irises with very large pupils. The whites of the eyes are not like those of humans, but have a pale gray cast. The ears are small and not low on the skull. The nose is thin and long, and the mouth is wider than in humans, and nearly lipless. There is no apparent facial hair and very little body hair, that being very fine and confined to the underarm and the groin area. The body is thin and without apparent body fat, but the muscles are well-developed. The hands are small, with four long digits but no opposable thumb. The outside digit is jointed in a manner as to be nearly opposable, and there is no webbing between the fingers as in humans. The legs are slightly but noticeably bowed, and the feet are somewhat splayed and proportionately large.

b. Type II. These entities are humanoid but differ from Type I in many respects. They are bi-pedal, 3 feet 5 inches to 4 feet 2 inches in height and weigh 25–50 pounds. Proportionately, the head is much larger than humans or Type I EBEs, the cranium being much larger and elongated. The eyes are very large, slanted and nearly wrap around the side of the skull. They are black with no whites showing. There is no noticeable brow ridge, and the skull has a slight peak that runs over the crown. The nose consists of two small slits which sit high above the slit-like mouth. There are no external ears. The skin is a pale bluish-gray color, being darker on the back of the creature, and is very smooth and fine-celled. There is no hair on either face or body, and these creatures do not appear to be mammalian. The arms are long in proportion to the legs, and the hands have three long, tapering fingers and a thumb which is nearly as long as the fingers. The second finger is thicker than the others, but not as long as the index finger. The feet are small and narrow, and four toes are joined together with a membrane.

It is not definitely known where either type of creature originated, but it seems certain that they did not evolve on earth. It is further evident, although not certain, that they may have originated on two different planets.

The Type II EBE bears a close resemblance to the alien bodies described by Glenn Dennis's friend on the autopsy table in Roswell in July 1947 (*see* chapter 2), although she did not describe any peak running over the crown of their heads.

If this document is authentic, I find it interesting and exciting for a number of reasons. First, it is incredible that the government of the USA should know about these little creatures and yet continue in public to deny their existence. And, secondly, it gives a form to the existence of these weird beings that sends a shiver down one's spine. It takes the discussion beyond the realm of the theoretical. It is like turning from a Walt Disney movie to find one's cat suddenly talking in a human voice.

THE BEGINNINGS OF MODERN UFOLOGY

There was a general awareness of UFOs over American skies during the month preceding the incident at Roswell. The first widely reported American UFO sighting occurred on 24 June 1947. Kenneth Arnold was flying his single-engined plane near Mount Rainier on his way to Yakima, Washington, for a business meeting. As the sky was clear, he put the plane in cruise control as he sat back and watched the beautiful scenery around him. Out of the corner of his eye he saw bright flashes of light – nine bright objects hovering about 9,500 feet above the ground. He estimated their speed at 1,700 mph as they headed from north to south, swerving and jinking between the high mountain peaks.

Arnold initially thought that they were search planes. As he kept watching, they travelled between Mount Rainier and Mount Adams, a distance of 47 miles. Every few seconds they would change course. As they turned, Arnold tried to see tails or wings, but there were none. His drawings of the objects after the event give the impression of boomerangs.

When he landed, he recounted his story to the press. He described the motion of the strange objects as like that of skimming saucers – 'saucer-like things . . . flying like geese in a diagonal chainlike line'. Bill Bequette, a reporter for a local newspaper, used the same phrase, and in so doing the two men gave birth to a new term for these strange craft: flying saucers.

Newspapers across the country quoted Bequette's story about Arnold's sighting. Nobody appeared to know what the objects were. Even the government was puzzled. The War Department, as it was then called, was particularly anxious to acquire for themselves craft that could fly with such speed and dexterity. Then reports of other sightings came flooding in to the media from all over the world. It was as if a dam had burst its banks. Arnold's experience encouraged people to report sightings, which they might previously have thought were hallucinations. Or had the first reports created a new fashion, with everyone trying to get in on the act without regard for the truth?

Newspapers tried to explain this new phenomenon, speculating on various explanations. Many scientists thought that the phenomenon was the result of a secret government research project.

There were three main theories that became popular. One was that the US Government was secretly producing new hexagonal-shaped aircraft, which at high speeds created the illusion of saucers. The second was that the objects were remote-controlled rockets. And the third suggested that a deep-cover scientific group had discovered a new form of travel, and that Kenneth Arnold had inadvertently observed one of their experiments.

There were several even stranger theories, one of which suggested that people were simply being confused by bright lights. Another suggested that the objects were meteors. This view took little account of the fact that the objects were able to move slowly and control their flight in a way that is beyond the capability of a meteor. Furthermore there were no known meteors falling towards the earth around this time.

One theory seemed to fit better than any of the others. This described the objects as spacecraft from another planet. The most popular suggestions at the time were Mars and Venus, but later the consensus was that they were from another solar system. The craft, it was suggested, were controlled by intelligent non-terrestrial beings.

The military seemed as mystified as everyone else. The weather balloon story was circulated to explain the incident two weeks later at Roswell, and for a while this became the accepted explanation. It soon became evident, however, that this was a mere cover story. Many people with inside information had the impression that Air Force pilots had instructions to attempt to capture one of these craft and its inhabitants.

SIGHTINGS AT THE TIME OF THE ROSWELL INCIDENT

The Roswell Incident received scant publicity at the time, since the story had been 'killed' by the military. But while it remained buried for more than 30 years, the plethora of other sightings in the summer of 1947 almost suggested an alien invasion of our airspace.

The day after Mac Brazel brought the pieces of debris into Sheriff George Wilcox's office in Roswell, while Lydia Sleppy at radio station KSWS was transmitting her story over the wire (*see* chapter 2), Vernon Baird saw a group of flying discs behind him, flying over the Tobacco Root Mountains, Montana. They were about 15 feet in diameter, and flying at 30,000 feet. They reminded him of yo-yos as he watched one of them break formation and fly directly towards him before it appeared to crash into the mountains.

THE SIGHTING AT BENTWATERS AIR FORCE BASE, SUFFOLK

In the 1980s Bentwaters was a US Air Force base which housed nuclear weapons. One day soon after Christmas 1980, unusual lights were seen in Rendlesham Forest, between Bentwaters and RAF Woodbridge, its British counterpart. On 13 January 1981, the Deputy Base Commander at Bentwaters, Lieutenant Colonel Halt, wrote the following account of these lights, copied to the Royal Air Force.

1 Early in the morning of 27 Dec 80 (approximately 0300L), two

USAF security police patrolmen saw unusual lights outside the back gate at RAF Woodbridge. Thinking an aircraft might have crashed or been forced down, they called for permission to go outside the gate to investigate. The on-duty flight chief responded and allowed three patrolmen to proceed on foot. The individuals reported seeing a strange glowing object in the forest. The object was described as being metalic [sic] in appearance and triangular in shape, approximately two to three meters across the base and approximately two meters high. It illuminated the entire forest with a white light. The object itself had a pulsing red light on top and a bank(s) of blue lights underneath. The object was hovering or on legs. As the patrolmen approached the object, it maneuvered though the trees and disappeared. At this time the animals on a nearby farm went into a frenzy. The object was briefly sighted approximately an hour later near the back gate.

2 The next day, three depressions 1½ inches deep and 7 inches in diameter were found where the object had been sighted on the ground. The following night (29 Dec 80) the area was checked for radiation. Beta/gamma readings of 0.1 milliroentgens were recorded with peak readings in the three depressions and near the center of the triangle formed by the depressions. A nearby tree had moderate (.05–.07) readings on the side of the tree toward the depressions.

3 Later in the night a red sun-like light was seen though the trees. It moved about and pulsed. At one point it appeared to throw off glowing particles and then broke into five separate white objects and then disappeared. Immediately thereafter, three star-like objects were noticed in the sky, two objects to the north and one to the south, all of which were about 10° off the horizon. The objects moved rapidly in sharp angular movements and displayed red, green and blue lights. The objects to the north appeared to be elliptical through an 8–12 power lens. They then turned to full circles. The objects to the north remained in the sky for an hour or more. The object to the south was visible for two or three hours and beamed down a stream of light from time to time. Numerous individuals, including the undersigned, witnessed the activities in paragraphs 2 and 3.

Charles I Halt, Lt Col, USAF
Deputy Base Commander

The first sighting

One of the three patrolmen referred to by Halt who were sent to investigate was Technical Sergeant Jim Penniston. He was tracked down by A J S Rayl who published an interview with him in *Omni* magazine in April 1994. He said:

> I was still pretty sure it was an aircraft downing at that point and asked Master Sergeant Chandler for permission to investigate. Master Sergeant Chandler contacted the shift commander's office, and within a minute or so I got the go-ahead to proceed off base with two other security policemen. We were told to leave our weapons behind, so as to not violate the Status Forces Agreement with the British. I and Airman First Class John Burroughs and Ed Cabansag, also an Airman First Class, got into our jeep and proceeded out the east gate, then down a logging road adjacent to the perimeter. It got too rocky, so we had to dismount the vehicle.

As they got to about 300 yards from the object, Penniston, saw blue, yellow and red pulsating lights. He paused to write in his notebook:

> Triangular in shape. The top portion is producing mainly white light, which encompasses most of the upper section of the craft. A small amount of white light peers out the bottom. At the left side center is a bluish light, and on the other side, red. The lights seem to be molded as part of the exterior of the structure, smooth, slowly fading into the rest of the outside of the structure, gradually molding into the fabric of the craft.

Since part of the role of perimeter security involved photographing people near the fence so that potential terrorists could be identified, Penniston had a camera with him, enabling him to photograph the object. But the pictures disappeared when the film was processed by the base processing laboratory.

After photographing the object, he continued towards it.

> I got to within 10 feet of the craft and the clearing where it sat. I estimated it to be about [6 feet high and 9 feet wide] at the base. No landing gear was apparent, but it seemed like she was on fixed legs. I moved a little closer. I had already taken all 36 pictures on

my roll of film. I walked around the craft, and finally, I walked right up to the craft. I noticed the fabric of the shell was more like a smooth, opaque, black glass. The bluish lights went from black to grey to blue. I was pretty much confused at that point. I kept trying to put this in some kind of frame of reference, trying to find some logical explanation as to what this was and what was going on. It was dead silent. No animals were even making noise anymore.

On the smooth exterior shell there was writing of some kind, but I couldn't quite distinguish it, so I moved up to it. It was 3 inch lettering, rather symbols, that stretched for the length of 2 feet, maybe a little more. I touched the symbols, and I could feel the shapes as if they were inscribed or etched or engraved, like a diamond cut on glass.

At that point, I backed away from the craft, because the light was starting to get brighter. Still, there was no sound. There was no physical contact with any kind of life form, but there did seem to be a life presence. It was mechanical, this ship, and it seemed to be under intelligent control.

A total of 80 people witnessed different aspects of this sighting, although none closer than Jim Penniston. Lieutenant Colonel Halt later commented: 'I personally knew the individuals. I knew they were very credible people.'

Jim Penniston was subsequently debriefed by two Office of Special Investigations investigators who with his agreement injected him with sodium pentathol to ensure that they gleaned a complete account of the incident from him. In 1994 when Penniston underwent regression hypnosis, 45 minutes of the encounter was unaccounted for. In the second of the two hypnotherapy sessions, he described the alien visitors as 'travellers from our future', each visiting the earth on a different task. Each team targeted certain people when it came back to our time, rather than just encountering people randomly. One of the visitors described his main task as obtaining human sperm, eggs and chromosomes in order to keep the human species alive. The world was described as darker, more polluted and colder. When David Jacobs, an abduction researcher, was asked for his opinion of this account, he said that Penniston appeared to have dropped into channelling mode.

The second sighting

Lieutenant Colonel Halt's report described events in the early hours of 27 December 1980. Two days later, in the early hours of 29 December, the phenomenon returned. Halt assembled a security team of 30 people who set out to investigate. With an audio tape recorder, Halt led his team into the forest with the aim of refuting any UFO claim.

> I certainly wasn't convinced it was a UFO, but I didn't know what it was and I wanted a logical explanation for what was going on. I'm certainly glad we made the tape, because if we hadn't made the tape even I would have trouble in believing what happened that night.

His words were caught on tape as they moved towards the lights.

> We see strange strobe-like flashes . . . rather sporadic but there's definitely something, some kind of phenomenon . . . We've got two strange objects . . . they're both heading north . . . Now we're observing what appears to be a beam coming down to the ground. This is unreal . . . the object to the south is still beaming down lights to the ground.

He later observed incredulously that the object

> . . . pulsated as though it were an eye winking at you, and around the edges it appeared to have molten metal dripping off it and falling to the ground. But I didn't see any evidence of it on the ground. I just couldn't believe what I was seeing. None of us could. Here I am a senior official who routinely denies this sort of thing and I'm involved in the middle of something I cannot explain . . .
>
> The object suddenly exploded, a silent explosion, and broke into three to five white objects and rapidly disappeared. As we moved out of the forest we noticed three objects in the sky. The objects in the sky were moving about – sharp angular movements, very high speed, as if they were looking for something. I kept

getting on the radio and called the Command Post. I wanted to know if they were finding anything on the radar scope. One of the objects in the sky was sending down beams – beams of lights, beams of energy, I'm not sure what they were. But at the same time I could hear on the radio voices talking about the beams coming down on the base ... At this stage my skepticism had definitely disappeared. I was really in awe.

A possible third sighting – the aliens are encountered

Larry Warren was on guard duty on the following night, and joined one of the teams that went into the forest to investigate. His account, however, is contradicted by that of Lieutenant Colonel Halt, who maintains that there were only two incidents, not three. Moreover, none of the other airmen substantiated Warren's story, which raises some doubts about its reality. Could it have been concocted after the event in order to cash in on a good story, as a result of having been in the right place at the right time?

According to Warren, he saw a red light move into a mist, followed by a blinding flash. When the mist cleared, he saw a large triangular craft with a white light on top. One of his group was filming the event, and as a shaft of light shone from the craft, they saw three entities inside it, which Warren described as small with enlarged heads and large dark eyes, with a semi-transparent appearance. They approached the Wing Commander, Colonel Williams, who stepped forward to meet them. There were no verbal communications or gestures. If there was any communication, it was telepathic. As the encounter continued, a noise in the forest caused the entities to withdraw slightly, but they resumed their previous position after a few moments.

One of the officers ordered the soldiers to return to their vehicles in the forest, where they had left their weapons in violation of the UK–USA Forces Agreement of which Larry Warren seems to be unaware. Suddenly a triangular craft, smaller than the main one appeared in the clearing where the trucks were parked. One of the officers grabbed the craft and was carried about 10 yards before releasing his grasp.

The men in Larry's group were too stunned to speak as they returned to the base. The next day however, they began to compare notes. The driver of one of the trucks said that one of the entities passed through the glass of his windscreen. In terror the driver described how he had kicked out the windshield with his boot. Others spoke about probes which passed through one of the trucks, from one side to the other.

Warren recalled British policemen taking photographs until one of the American officers confiscated their cameras, but Halt pointed out that since the US Air Force was a guest in another country, he had no authority outside the airbase, and he would not therefore risk interfering with the police of the host country. His observation casts some doubt on Larry Warren's story.

The airman who filmed the event was later flown to a US Air Force base in Germany. He later heard that Lieutenant Colonel Halt had made a four hour running commentary of it. The next day all those who had witnessed the event were extensively debriefed. They all signed a previously prepared statement and were instructed to speak to nobody about what had happened.

Warren made a reversed-charge call to his mother in the USA from a payphone at the base. As he began to tell her about his experience, the line went dead. The US operator informed him that the call had been disconnected by the base. He was later questioned about the call and a recording of his disconnected conversation was replayed to him by security officers.

Most of the airmen who were witnesses to the event were posted abroad shortly afterwards and Larry Warren left the Air Force a few months later in May 1981. In order to make sense of his experience and to overcome his uneasiness about it, he contacted a UFO organization with whom he shared the story. He has also written his own account of the event in his book, *Left at East Gate*.

Comment by Britain's former Chief of Defence Staff

Lord Peter Hill-Norton, former Chief of the British Defence
Staff, later commented on the events at Bentwaters as follows:

> It seems to me that something physical took place, that something
> landed at this US Air Force base. And I have no doubt that it got
> the people concerned at the base, including the Commanding
> General, into a very considerable state . . . Either large numbers
> of people, including the Commanding General at Bentwaters,
> were hallucinating, and for an American Air Force nuclear base
> this is extremely dangerous, or what they say happened did
> happen.

AN ENCOUNTER IN STEPHEN, MINNESOTA

Chris Rutkowski was at home in Winnipeg, Manitoba, Canada
on 27 August 1979 when he heard a report on a local radio
station about an encounter with a UFO just across the US
border in the north-eastern corner of Minnesota, within the
investigation range of the UFO Research Organization of
Manitoba, the local UFO organization. He contacted Guy
Westcott, a close associate, who was on holiday in Minnesota. Westcott interviewed the man who had experienced the
encounter, Deputy Sheriff Val Johnson of the town of Stephen,
Minnesota. He returned with a detailed report and tape
recording of the interview.

> This is Deputy Sheriff Val Johnson. I report in connection with
> an incident which happened August 27th, 1979, at approximately
> 1.40 am, western section of Marshall County, approximately 10
> miles west of Stephen, Minnesota. This officer was on routine
> patrol, westbound down Marshall County Road 5. I got to the
> intersection of 5 and Minnesota State 220. When I looked down
> south on 220 to check for traffic, I noticed a very bright,
> brilliant light, 8–12 inches in diameter, 3–4 feet off the ground.
> The edges were very defined. I thought perhaps at first that it
> could be an aircraft in trouble, as it appeared to be a landing light
> from an aircraft. I proceeded south on 220. I proceeded about a
> mile and three tenths or a mile and four tenths when the light

intercepted my vehicle causing damage to a headlight, putting a dent in the hood, breaking the windshield and bending antennae on top of the vehicle. At this point, at the interception of the light, Iwas rendered either unconscious, neutralized or unknowing for a period of approximately 39 minutes. From the point of intersection, my police vehicle proceeded south in a straight line 854 feet, at which point the brakes were engaged by forces unknown to myself, as I do not remember doing this, and I left about approximately 99 feet of black marks on the highway before coming to rest sideways in the road with the grille of my hood facing in an easterly direction. At 2.19 am, I radioed a 10–88 [Officer Needs Assistance] to my dispatcher in Warren. He dispatched an officer from Stephen who came out, ascertained the situation as best he could, called for the Stephen Ambulance to transport me to Warren Hospital for further tests, X-rays and observation. At the time the officer arrived, I complained about having very sore eyes. At Warren Hospital, it was diagnosed that I had a mild case of welder's burns to my eyes. My eyes were treated with some salve and adhesive bandages put over and I was instructed to keep them on for the remainder of the day, or approximately 24 hours. At 11.00 am, Sheriff Dennis Breckie, my employer, picked me up at my residence in Oslo, and transported me to an ophthalmologist in Grand Forks, North Dakota. He examined my eyes and said I had some irritation to the inner portions of the eye which could have been caused by seeing a bright light after dark. That is all I have to add except to say that my timepiece in the police vehicle and my mechanical wrist watch were both lacking 14 minutes of time to the minute.

When Everett Doolittle, the officer sent to help Johnson, found his colleague slumped forward over the steering wheel and in a state of mild shock. A bruise later appeared on Johnson's forehead, caused possibly by impact with the steering wheel. Johnson was dazed, and said that 'everything was in slow motion'. He had an 'excruciating' pain in the eyes, which he described as like that from a welding torch.

'It was as if someone had hit me in the face with a 400-pound pillow,' he said of the sensation he felt in his head. A dental examination one week after his experience showed damage to his bridgework, which was broken at the gums.

The physical evidence and the missing 14 minutes

When Doolittle arrived on the scene, Johnson's police car was front end first in the left-hand ditch. The impact point was determined by the location of the broken glass of the headlight on the road, 953 feet from where the car was found. From that point, yaw marks (described as faint skid marks caused by putting a car out of gear without applying the brakes) travelled in a straight line for 854 feet down the road. These became dark skid marks from there to where the car stopped moving, going in a straight line for most of the remaining length, and turning abruptly at the end toward the ditch.

The right member of the left pair of headlights was broken. There was a round dent, approximately 1 inch in diameter on the bonnet, directly over the master brake cylinder. It looked as if a hammer had struck the hood at an angle between 45 and 75 degrees from the horizontal. A photograph taken with a UV filter showed that there was a deposit left on the flat surface at the bottom of the dent.

The windscreen had an interesting pattern of breakage, in the shape of a teardrop with the point up, on the driver's side. Three main impact points were visible, although the lowest of the three was the largest and most complex. Tests on the glass by the Ford Motor Company suggested that there were signs of both inward and outward motion of the windscreen. The company was apparently unfamiliar with such a breakage pattern. Impact from an object such as a small stone would have caused the windscreen to shatter even at a relatively low speed, so it is hard to interpret the shattering as an actual impact. Analytical findings bear some resemblance to those of a shock-wave-induced breakage.

The roof light had its glass knocked out and the police radio antenna on the centre of the roof was bent, about 5 inches up from the roof, at a 45 degree angle. The CB antenna on the boot was bent near its tip, at an angle of almost 90 degrees, 3 inches from the top.

The police investigators observed that all the damage on the vehicle occurred in a straight path no more wider than 12 inches wide. Because of this linear formation, it was suggested that an object had struck a glancing blow to the car, initially hitting the headlight, then rolling over the bonnet, up the window and over the roof. But this explanation could not account for all the damage as it was found. An object hitting the car at the front would not be able to redirect its force downward further up the bonnet, graze the window and still have enough force to bend the antennae.

The antennae were spring loaded, so anything bending them would have to have been travelling extremely fast to create the shape to which they were bent. It was suggested that they were bent by a strong deceleration, causing them to whip forward. But their design is such that they can withstand a strong deceleration without acute bending. Any deceleration of sufficient strength to bend them backwards as they moved forward might have killed the occupant. Most curiously, the dead insects which had adhered to the antennae were not wiped off from the impact, as might be expected.

The battery of the car could no longer hold a charge. It has been suggested that the headlight and roof light were imploded by a high-energy electrical source, and ball lightning was suggested as a cause. But ball lightning could not have created the dent in the bonnet or the impacts on the windscreen, nor could it have bent the antennae. The electric clock in the car was found to be missing 14 minutes, and also, more strangely, was Johnson's mechanical wristwatch. This is indeed odd, because both were synchronized with the clocks in the police station earlier in the night, and all time checks after that agreed, as late as 01.00, only a short while before the incident.

The CB radio in the car was not in good working condition prior to the incident, but it was described as 'even worse' afterwards.

Allan Hendry of the Center for UFO Studies sent a gauss-meter to the police investigators, in order for them to test for changes in the car's magnetic pattern, but there were none. Finally, there was evidence of dust particles in the shattered glass, and it was suggested that this dust was the residue found in the round dent in the bonnet.

The psychological effects

When Val Johnson called for help, his voice was described as being 'weak', and like 'someone coming out of a daze'. He had apparently been unconscious for 39 minutes, from the time he heard glass breaking and felt the light 'hit' him, to the time he opened one eye to see the red ignition light on his dashboard. During that period, the car had travelled in a straight line for 953 feet, before veering to the left, over the left lane and into the ditch. Johnson does not remember applying the brakes, yet the skid marks indicate that they were definitely applied.

When Johnson was asked what he thought had happened to him, he said that he believed he 'had seen something [that he] wasn't supposed to see'. He speculated that his sight had been temporarily neutralized to prevent him from seeing whatever he had stumbled across. He declined invitations to undergo regression hypnosis, despite a substantial financial inducement, declaring that he was 'not curious' about what had happened to him. He concluded by saying that whereas as he had previously been sceptical about UFOs, 'I am now committed', and that if he ever saw that light again, he would stop the car and 'yell for help!'

SOCORRO, NEW MEXICO: A CLOSE ENCOUNTER OF THE THIRD KIND

On 24 April 1964, police officer Lonnie Zamora was on his way to investigate a reported explosion in a rural area outside Socorro, New Mexico. As he approached the area he saw an egg-shaped craft on four thin legs, and two small humanoid figures in white overall-type outfits. He saw the figures enter the craft which flew off moments before his back-up, Sergeant Sam Chavez, arrived. Both Zamora and Chavez went to the landing site, where they found physical evidence of the visit.

This is undoubtedly one of the best-documented and best-attested CE3 cases on record. Even a classified memo to the CIA, recently declassified, mentioned it as the 'best' of its kind that Project Blue Book, an investigation into UFO sightings by the Air Force, ever found. It is a case in which the facts clearly support the claims of the witnesses. The incident was investigated by Ray Stanford of the National Investigations Committee on Aerial Phenomena, who arrived in Socorro within four days of the event. His account is documented in *Socorro 'Saucer' in a Pentagon Pantry*. Chris Lambright investigated further, and after talking to Zamora, he has produced a diagram of the site, and a painting of the craft and the symbol on the side of the craft.

Socorro is a small town, 70 miles south of Albuquerque. Lonnie Zamora had just finished chasing a speeding car when he was told to check on an explosion on the edge of town. Thinking that a small shack containing dynamite may have exploded, he drove cautiously up a rough embankment and slowly along a narrow gravel road that wound its way beside a small arroyo (a shallow dry gully). He saw what he thought was an overturned car in the arroyo about 150–200 yards away. He described what looked like two children or small adults, one of which seemed startled at his approach and 'jump[ed] somewhat'.

He drove further along the gravel road, then stopped and reported to the sheriff's office that he was about to leave his vehicle, 'checking the car down in the arroyo'. He then heard several loud 'thumps' or 'slams', like metal hitting metal. After a few steps, he saw an elongated oval-shaped object on 'girder-like' legs. At that moment a loud roar and bluish flame shot out of the underside of the object as it began to rise. Zamora dropped to the ground thinking the object was about to explode. He got up and ran to the other side of the gravel road, behind his own vehicle, knocking off his spectacles in the process.

He heard a whirring noise and the object rose up out of the arroyo. The legs he had seen moments before were no longer visible. The object was aluminum-white with a red insignia on the side – about 2.5 feet high and 2 feet wide. He noted that the object had risen to perhaps 20 feet above the bottom of the gully when suddenly the sound stopped completely. The flame was no longer visible and he watched as the now-silent vehicle moved off parallel to the terrain, picking up speed as it left the area. He watched it move off into the distance and it eventually disappeared from view.

Almost immediately after the object had left the area, Sergeant Sam Chavez arrived, having overheard Zamora radioing wildly to his dispatcher in the hope that someone else might be able to see the object. Together they noted the evidence left in the arroyo – a half-burned bush, four angular impressions in the sandy soil where the 'legs' had been, and several small footprints and other impressions.

The verdict of the former head of Project Blue Book

In 1966 Hector Quintanilla Jr, former head of Project Blue Book, wrote about Lonnie Zamora's experience in *Studies in Intelligence*.

> There is no doubt that Lonnie Zamora saw an object which left quite an impression on him. There is also no question about Zamora's reliability. He is a serious police officer, a pillar of his church, and a man well versed in recognizing airborne vehicles in his area. He is puzzled by what he saw, and frankly, so are we. This is the best-documented case on record, and still we have been unable, in spite of thorough investigation, to find the vehicle or other stimulus that scared Zamora to the point of panic.

This document was approved for release on 2 January 1981 and is available under the provisions of the Freedom of Information Act.

CATTLE MUTILATIONS

Since the 1960s, animals all over the world have been found lying dead in fields with their bodies mutilated, but with no blood, tracks or signs of struggle around them. The marks found on the animals are not consistent with attacks by predators such as wolves or coyotes. Instead, the incisions and the removal of internal organs have been done with great surgical precision, and in some cases there is evidence that high heat (perhaps from a high-powered laser) has been used to cut the tissues. It has also been found that the animals have been totally drained of blood. And in many cases the owners heard nothing during the night.

Typical cattle mutilations have involved huge oval incisions around the jaw bone. In most cases the exposed jaw has been completely removed and the tongue cut out with a precise incision deep in the throat. In addition, at least one eyeball has been removed, as has the udder in cows. The sexual organs on both sexes are also invariably removed. All removals and incisions have been performed with care and precision. In some cases the evidence of cauterization along the incision lines has led investigators to believe that some form of intensely hot cutting device has been used, strongly suggesting a laser. Bones have also been cut cleanly with no bone fragments around the cut.

UFOs and strange, black, unmarked helicopters have been linked with these mutilations. They have been sighted at the same time in the area where mutilated bovines have been found. Black helicopters are rumoured to be used by the special US government teams employed to hunt extraterrestrials.

No one has ever been associated with or convicted of any of these bizarre acts. But why, one might ask, should extra-terrestrials be interested in cattle? The answer may lie in the fact that cattle blood is similar to human blood, and is regularly used to create human blood plasma.

Alabama incidents

In November 1992, the Fyffe Police Department, Alabama, conducted an investigation into unexplained cattle mutilations in co-operation with neighbouring police and law enforcement agencies.

More than 30 animals were discovered dead in pastures with various internal and external organs missing. The incisions showed a precise surgical cut. In many cases there was evidence of intense heat at the tissue excisions. But although many of the dead animals were found in soft pasture land and in mud, there were no footprints, tracks or marks found anywhere near the mutilated animals. No suspects were found, nor any motives for these incidents of phantom surgery. And no witness or informant came forward to offer any credible insight or testimony.

The first documented incident was reported on 20 October 1992 by Albertville cattle farmer John Strawn. The animal was discovered in a wooded area of Mr Strawn's pasture by a neighbour who found it lying on its side. Its entire milk sac was missing with no evidence of blood on the animal or on the ground around where it lay. The neighbour said the neat, oval incision where the udder had been removed appeared to be charred.

Other farmers in the area soon started reporting similar cases over the next two months. The same organs were reported missing, although what was taken varied from animal to animal. In many cases the rectum had been cored out neatly, with no evidence of blood or body fluid present. On female livestock the sex organs had been removed in an identical fashion with clean, bloodless excisions. On male livestock, the sex organs had also been removed, again in oval, bloodless excisions.

In early January, Albertville Police Department's Chief of Detectives, Tommy Cole, reported that his ranch, too, had fallen victim to the mutilators when an Angus steer fell prey to the phantom surgeons. It was at that point that the Fyffe Police Department began working closely with the Albertville Police Department to investigate further the continuing incidents of mutilations.

A week later, the mutilators struck again in Albertville. The following week mutilated cattle were reported near Fyffe, in Grove Oak. A week later the vandals had moved to Dawson, just outside Fyffe. During the first week of February 1993, more than nine cases of cattle mutilation were reported in Marshall and DeKalb counties.

Throughout the period that the cases were reported, cattle farmers and their neighbours saw helicopters in the vicinity either before or shortly after mutilated cattle were discovered.

It is rumoured that MJ-12 teams whose task is to capture alien life forms, use black helicopters.

Oklahoma incidents

Two mutilated black cattle were also found dead in fields about 60 miles apart, in Canadian and Blaine counties, Oklahoma, following a full moon. They had their sexual organs removed. Mustang Police Chief Ron Lewis said his office had investigated the mutilation of a 1,100-pound Angus cow. Blaine County Under-sheriff Kent Sexton said his office was called to the ranch of Galen Slagell near Hydro the same morning to investigate the mutilation of a 700-pound Angus steer. Although Lewis admitted that he was not versed in the ways of cults, he thought some type of cult celebration coinciding with Passover might be responsible for the mutilations. Both investigations turned up similarities. No blood was found at the scene of either mutilation, and Lewis and Sexton said both cattle appeared to be 'drained of blood'. The interior and exterior sex organs, tongues and one eye from each animal had been removed. The cow found in Canadian County was missing her left ear and a patch of hide over her ribs on the right side.

The cow's owner, who asked not to be identified, said he had checked his cattle the evening before the mutilation. 'I had just worked them and I knew I didn't have any sick ones. When I went to check them, I saw her and I knew she was dead by the way she was lying.' He initially thought that the cow had been shot and then vandalized by coyotes. A closer examination showed that the mutilation was not the work of coyotes. There were some drops of blood on the ground, but none from the wounds. He said this was odd because when someone shoots a cow, a death struggle occurs, resulting in a pool of blood. There were no tracks, human or animal, around the carcass. 'When I walked up, I left tracks,' he said. He checked the animal carefully but was unable to identify the cause of death.

Under-sheriff Sexton noted that it had rained before the

steer was found and the ground was soft, but 'there were no prints.' He was familiar with cattle, and commented 'this wasn't coyotes'. Ranch owner Slagell agreed: 'I don't know of any coyotes that carry knives.' Tim Lowry, the vet, could find no bullet hole. 'We're baffled,' declared Sexton. According to Lowry, 'There definitely was a human hand involved.' Slagell said he was still not ruling out the possibility that the mutilation could have been done by vultures, but the Blaine County Assistant District Attorney, George Burnett, said the steer 'obviously was surgically cut'.

10,000 mutilations in 48 states in 30 years

Law enforcement agency reports covering 48 states in the USA since 1963 show that the cases recently documented in north-eastern Alabama are part of a wider national problem. More than 10,000 cases of livestock mutilations have been reported since 1967, and in every case the same organs and tissues were removed. Sex organs were taken and tongues were cut with an incision made deep in the throat. Eyes and ears were also removed. The jaw was stripped to the bone in a large oval cut. Rectums were removed, almost as if a stovepipe had been inserted and muscle and tissue cored out.

This massive slaughter has been achieved with no evidence of spilt blood at the point of incision. And the entire blood supply of each animal has been drained without cardiovascular collapse.

Residents and public officials have offered many explanations. Some believe the mutilations are the work of predators such as coyotes or buzzards. Another belief is that they were done by a satanic cult or college students. But scientists who have analysed material collected from the animals clearly rule out both possibilities.

4

ABDUCTIONS

Abduction by alien beings is a recent phenomenon in the field of ufology. It refers to people who are removed against their will to some place away from earth and have something unusual done to them. They are usually returned to, or close to, the place from which they were abducted. The experience is invariably unpleasant for the abductees – primarily because of the powerlessness they experience. These are close encounters of the fourth kind (CE4).

The abductions may have been taking place for longer than we realize. It is possible that it has only recently been brought to public attention because heightened awareness of matters affecting the psyche is a relatively recent phenomenon.

Abductions are about small grey humanoids removing people for reasons that are still unclear. Most appear to involve medical-physiological examinations, in which sperm and egg cells are removed from the victims. In order to cloak their activities the aliens are able to create a hypnotic state so that very few people have any conscious recollection of what has been done to them. Some people *are* able to consciously recall their experiences, but in most cases the abductors appear to insert a memory block into the minds of the abductees, inhibiting them from doing so. Even in these cases, however, the victims are left with a feeling of discomfort or unease that provides a clue. Regression therapy has become an accepted way to uncover the events which have been lying in their unconscious.

In a recent survey quoted by Richard Hall in his excellent book *Uninvited Guests*, he analyses 19 abductions across seven countries, from houses, vehicles and out in the open. Two thirds of the abductees could not initially recall the experience and three quarters later discovered that they had undergone a physical examination. All of these had needle-like probes inserted into their bodies. One third of the sample were returned to a different location from where they were abducted and almost two thirds were given messages about the future of mankind.

The main question that arises is: why are they doing it? What do they want with us? There are a plethora of theories. There are even those who question the sanity of people who claim to have been abducted. A large body of opinion holds that abductions are psychological phenomena which take place primarily in the minds of the 'abductees'. Another view is that abductions are a new kind of dream state, like a shamanic journey. Dr Kenneth Ring argues in *The Omega Project* that the abduction phenomenon is a manifestation of the development of a more advanced form of humanity. In support of this contention, he quotes Michael Grosso, who observes in *The Final Choice* that 'our continued survival as a species lies in our being able to develop a deeper awareness of our transcendental nature' and that we are 'spiritual beings who are gradually becoming aware of our spiritual essence'.

The most effective therapy for many abductee, which seems to minimize the disturbance and bring some sense of equilibrium to them, has been regression therapy. This involves taking a person back to a disturbing event and having them re-experience their emotions. Acknowledgment of what has taken place has long been recognized as one of the best forms of therapy.

MICHELLE LAVIGNE'S CLASSIFICATION OF ABDUCTIONS

One of the most useful guides for assisting abductees is Michelle LaVigne's book, *The Alien Abduction Survival Guide*. It is the most comprehensive insight that I have come across into the greys and their methods. In it, LaVigne divides abductions into three main groups: the one-time incident, the quick in-and-out and the Gemini people, who are involved with the extraterrestrials in an ongoing collaboration programme.

The 'one-timers' are picked up from various locations and deposited back on earth after some genetic material has been drawn from them. Such people usually have no recollection of what has happened to them. The 'in-and-outers' are usually collected from their beds at night on different occasions, for an hour or two each time. Evidence of this abduction involves bleeding from their ears or nose and cuts or scars. Much of this physical evidence has disappeared by morning, although occasionally a faint white scar may be visible the next day. Such people are rigidly controlled by their abductors and usually have only a slight memory of their night-time experiences.

LaVigne refers to the regular abductees as Gemini people because of the double lives they lead – they have jobs assigned to them by their abductors which they carry out on the space-craft. Indeed, she prefers the word 'experiencer' to 'abductee' since the Gemini people are highly skilled in their ability to use their psychic senses to feel and reflect the emotions of others.

The jobs assigned to these Gemini people vary. 'Teachers' conduct classes and one-on-one sessions. Their pupils are mainly 'halflings' – the word that LaVigne uses for hybrids who are half extraterrestrial and half human, the result of the cross-fertilization of human and alien cells. The one-on-one sessions are conducted with gifted earthlings, with the aim of teaching them self-realization and insight. Four small, metallic grey balls are used. 'Each ball, from top down, raises the intensity of the vision revealed to its holder.'

'Child-care givers' have a maternal or paternal role, pro-viding the hybrid children with love, care and attention. They are models with whom the hybrid children are able to bond by playing games and telling stories.

The role of 'empaths' is to control, restrain and subdue problem individuals. They have a naturally calming effect on other people. Fear and panic will cause many abductees to break away and run around the spaceship looking for a way out. This is understandable, but when their fears are expressed in a violent manner, they are likely to attack the aliens and cause injury to themselves, to hybrids and to other abductees. There are also unsafe areas in a ship that can cause severe burns to the rogue individual.

Empaths have a wand that can be used somewhat like a cattle prod. 'It can induce searing pain at just a touch, particularly if the touch is to a temple, wrist or ankle . . . [and another] type . . . can deliver a stunning shock that immobilizes the target', although the empaths are usually able to subdue anxious abductees by their soothing ways. Their role clearly highlights the powerlessness of the abductees. It reminds one of the way that humans treat animals.

'Full-timers' are permanent residents of the alien world who originated on earth; many of them are missing twins. Finally, the role of 'astral-abductees' is the most challenging to traditional beliefs about reality. According to LaVigne, this type of collaborator is a soul-traveller who regularly leaves his or her body on earth and temporarily inhabits an alien or human host body on an alien base or spaceship.

FOUR WELL-KNOWN ABDUCTIONS

I will now describe four well-known abductions in some detail in order thereafter to explore the ultimate purpose of the alien abductors.

The first recorded case of someone taken aboard a UFO against their will is Antonio Villas Boas, who was dragged from his tractor while working on his farm in Brazil in 1957. At the time his story sounded incredible, although he had radiation burns and a scar where a blood sample was taken.

The most widely recorded abduction cases are those of Betty and Barney Hill in 1961 and Betty Andreasson in 1967. The Hills' story has been popularized by Budd Hopkins in his book *Intruders*, and presented in even greater detail by John Fuller in *The Interrupted Journey*. Betty Andreasson's story and its implications have been examined in increasing detail by Raymond Fowler in *The Andreasson Affair* and *The Andreasson Affair, Phase Two*. He further amplified the theme in his later books, *The Watchers: The Secret Design Behind the UFO Abductions* and *The Watchers II*.

Travis Walton's story of his abduction in 1975 was made into a successful film, *Fire in the Sky*. Although his abduction is in itself dramatic, his recollection of what took place inside the spacecraft is patchy, and the film uses a degree of cinematographic licence to fill in some of the detail.

Antonio Villas Boas, 1957, Brazil

On 14 October 1957, a Brazilian farmer named Antonio Villas-Boas and his brother were ploughing a field on his family's ranch when they saw a bright red light hovering over a field. Antonio moved towards the light, which moved each time he approached it. It eventually disappeared.

The next evening the object landed in front of him and bathed him and his tractor in a bright red light. The red light changed to green, and a series of lights that revolved around the middle of the craft slowed down as the craft landed. It was dish-shaped with a flattened dome on top and three support legs which emerged as it approached the ground.

The tractor's engine and ignition system died – electro-mechanical failure has since been observed as a feature when UFOs are in the vicinity. Villas Boas attempted to jump from his tractor and run away. Three creatures who were shoulder-height to Villa Boas and who wore tight-fitting silver suits and helmets caught him and carried him struggling up a ramp into the craft. The door was closed after them; it was so tight-fitting that no seam was visible.

His abductors spoke in barks like dogs as he was forcibly undressed and covered with a clear liquid which quickly dried. Following this he was taken into another room where he underwent a physical examination. Later, a beautiful, naked, almost human-looking woman approached him. She had blonde hair, a wide face, a pointed chin, elongated blue eyes and thin lips. She caressed and aroused him, and this led to sexual intercourse – twice – which he enjoyed until the woman began to grunt like an animal. One of his abductors returned and ordered the woman to leave. She pointed to Villas Boas, then to her stomach and finally upwards to the sky.

He was then given back his clothes and taken on a tour of the ship. He tried to take a piece of equipment to prove that he had been there, but his abductors angrily stopped him. He was released shortly afterwards as they grunted among themselves. The entire episode lasted four and a quarter hours.

After an initial period of exhaustion he suffered from extreme lethargy for a month. Strange marks and wounds also appeared on his hands and arms. They were diagnosed as radiation poisoning, but with no long-term effects. Villas Boas went on to qualify as a lawyer and stuck to his story, which he never changed or varied, until his dying day.

Betty and Barney Hill, 1961, Portsmouth, New Hampshire

In September 1961 Betty and Barney Hill were driving home from a holiday in Canada on a deserted road, less than 2 miles from North Woodstock, New Hampshire. They saw an object that looked like a bright star pacing their car. Radar operators at Pease Air Force Base nearby subsequently confirmed that something was moving in the air in their vicinity at the time reported by the Hills.

Barney stopped the car several times so that his wife could study the object through a pair of binoculars. It had various flashing lights, and they thought it was an aeroplane or helicopter. It curved around and came towards them, taking up a position in front of the car before moving slightly off the road and hovering. They stopped their car to have a closer look after Betty saw through the binoculars that it was shaped like a disc.

Barney took the binoculars and got out of the car for a closer look. He could see portholes on the craft, through which he saw several humanoid figures who appeared to be working busily and looking at them. He quickly returned to the car and drove off down the road as fast as possible feeling somewhat drowsy.

They arrived home safely, or so they thought, but later, events took a strange turn. Barney noticed that there were blotches on the paintwork of his car and his shoes were scuffed. They were also unable to account for two hours; missing time has become one of the recognition signals of an abduction. Moreover, their journey was 35 miles shorter than it should have been.

Two weeks after the sighting, Betty began to have nightmares about UFOs and aliens. As these dreams began to disturb her, she visited a psychologist. Under hypnosis, she remembered being taken aboard the spacecraft and being physically examined. Barney told a similar tale, although it was different in several details. Their psychologist came to the conclusion that they were remembering a similar dream, but the Hills disagreed. They thought that they were remembering what actually happened on that night, although sceptics subsequently suggested that the dream was inspired by Betty's reading and seeing a popular film about aliens.

The couple decided to seek more professional help and were referred by their doctor to Dr Benjamin Simon, a Boston psychiatrist, in December 1963 to try hypnotic regression therapy. Barney Hill's session was recorded on audio tape. Under hypnosis, he recalled being led up a ramp into the ship and into a type of examination room. He was lying on a table where he could feel hands examining him. They completed a fairly thorough examination and he was led out of the room, down the ramp and back to the car, where his wife was waiting. She came around and opened the car door for him.

His wife's recollections were similar. She told of an examination and also of one of the crew members who seemed to speak English. She believed that a picture was taken of her skin and a sample collected for later study. Further, she claimed that she was also examined internally by the use of a needle inserted into her navel. This added to Dr Simon's scepticism and he noted that there was no such medical procedure. Yet just such a procedure was introduced some years later.

When Betty asked the leader where they came from, he showed her a star map which she was able to replicate under

hypnosis. It depicted two large stars with several lines drawn
between them, which the entity told her were 'trade routes'.
A score of smaller stars were scattered about the drawing.
Some year later, a teacher and amateur astronomer named
Marjorie Fish correlated the drawing with a known section of
space, including stars that had not yet been charted at the time
of the Hills' abduction. It placed the aliens as coming from a
star system known as Zeta Reticuli – which matches information provided by channeller Lyssa Royal.

Betty Andreasson, 1967, Ashburnham, Massachusetts

The story of Betty Andreasson, a Massachusetts housewife,
began in August 1975 when she saw an article in her local
newspaper. Dr J Allen Hynek, founder and director of the
Center for UFO Studies, was looking for people who had
encountered UFOs. Her case was eventually investigated
seventeen months later in January 1977 by MUFON investigator Jules Vailancourt. Mindful of the usefulness of hypnotic
regression in the recent case of Betty and Barney Hill, Henry
J Edelson of the New England Institute of Hypnosis was
recruited to help uncover Betty Andreasson's buried memories.
Her remarkable story unfolded over fourteen hypnotic
regression sessions between April and July 1977, which took
her back to 25 January, 1967, ten years earlier when Betty was
30 years old.

Betty was at her home in Ashburnham, Massachusetts with
her parents and children, when her father, Waino Aho,
reported seeing a light outside the kitchen window. Peering
out of the pantry window, he saw strange little creatures with
over-sized heads approaching the house. He later described
them in a signed statement as looking like Halloween freaks.
Four or five entities came into the house through the closed
wooden kitchen door. They had large almond-shaped eyes that
wrapped around their heads, and left a vapour trail behind
them as they floated forward. They were between three and a
half and four and a half feet tall. Their leader who introduced
himself to Betty as Quazgaa – her phonetic rendition of his

name – was slightly taller than his companions. He communicated telepathically with Betty, who misunderstood the communication and offered them food. She began to cook some meat which began to burn. Quazgaa clarified the situation, saying telepathically that their kind of food is 'tried by fire, knowledge tried by fire.' Betty has strong Christian beliefs and offered Quazgaa her bible. She received a thin blue book from him in exchange. Despite the detail of Betty's story, it seems to be discredited by some ufologists – perhaps because of the spiritual element, which later emerged. Many ufologists reject any explanation of UFOs and extraterrestrial encounters that does not treat them as purely physical phenomena.

In the meantime, the visitors had put Betty's entire family into a suspended state, as if time had stopped. Betty's daughter, Becky recovered and awoke. Later, under hypnosis, she was able to recall the incident. She described the shiny, dark blue, tight-fitting uniform worn by the visitors. Their trousers appeared to merge into their boots. She noticed that her visitors had club-like hands with three thick fingers, unlike the greys who are described as having four long, thin, spidery fingers. Becky described them as having upside-down pear shaped heads without hair, eyes like marbles, orifices instead of a nose or ears, and a slit or a scar for a mouth, like a wrinkle in their clay-like skin. Although similar in size and appearance to the greys, Quazgaa and his fellows seem to be of a different species to them. Their clay-like skin is different to the scaled skin of the greys.

When Quazgaa noticed Becky, he stared at her and she lapsed back into unconsciousness. With enormous presence of mind, despite feeling tranquillized by the visitors, Betty asked them what they wanted. In the interchange, Quazgaa asked Betty for her help, saying that they had come to help because the world is trying to destroy itself. When he asked Betty to follow them, she asked about the well-being of her family. After reassuring Betty about her family, Quazgaa persuaded Betty to join them. This is unlike most abduction scenarios in which the abductors remove their victims without any dialogue, and usually ignore completely questions that are put to them. The greys are more insistent in their physical examinations and their human breeding programme. Quazgaa's people, as we shall see, had on this occasion a very different agenda in mind.

During the hypnosis sessions Betty was reliving every detail of the episode, the memory of which was otherwise unavailable to her. Once the memory block was removed from her mind, Betty was able after the hypnosis sessions to recall these events without further assistance. Her experience is as outlandish as a dream, although dreams never seem to have the detailed clarity and consistency of Betty's story. Furthermore, once we recall a dream, we know that it was a dream. Once Betty was able to recall the actual experience, it had a reality for her that is not the product of a dream experience.

Quazgaa gently commanded Betty to stand in line behind him while one of his companions stood directly behind her, and they floated out through the wooden kitchen door. Betty was surprised at seeing an oval object with a raised central console standing in a foggy haze in her backyard. In order to reassure Betty, Quazgaa made the bottom of the craft temporarily transparent so that she was able to see some of the objects inside. She noted that they were illustrated in the blue book that she had been given by Quazgaa.

Betty provided a full description of the inside of the craft, as recounted in *The Andreasson Affair*. Her descriptions are further enhanced by a number of very detailed drawings – a tribute to Betty's ability as a graphics artist. Her drawings contribute considerably to our understanding of extra-terrestrials and their technology.

She described the drive mechanism in the bottom of the craft as consisting of three or four large glass balls which were connected to a neck-like structure so that they look like translucent bulbous skittles as used in ten-pin bowling. These were connected by the neck to three or four horizontal glass wheels. The balls and the wheels together rotate in a horizontal plane in a circular mechanism that looks like a glass rim. The balls generate the red, green and blue, and sometimes white, pulsating colours, often associated with UFOs. The rotation somehow causes a vacuum, or suction effect, as in a tornado, which seems to power the craft. Another interesting feature is that the legs of the craft, which was on the side of the hill, were of differing lengths, enabling it to remain on an even keel. The doorway to the craft which opened as they approached, as Quazgaa raised his hand, could not otherwise be seen. The outer door and all inner doorways, as reported by all abductees on other spacecraft, fit flush with the body of the craft – there is never any visible join.

After some preparatory treatment, Betty was eventually led to the examining room where the aliens noted that some of Betty's body parts were missing. Presumably they were referring to the hysterectomy which she had undergone. A long needle with a tube on the end was inserted into Betty's abdomen via her navel. Betty became distressed as she felt the tube moving about inside her. Quazgaa, who was not the examining physician, put his hand on Betty's forehead and relieved the pain. They also inserted a long thin needle into Betty's left nasal passage and removed a miniature spiked ball the size of an airgun pellet. She was also examined by a large light that looked like an eye with a lens in the middle. Quazgaa then waved his hands over Betty's hands and legs, whereupon she began to float above the examining table, and into a standing position.

She was then led through a dressing room to another room which was in the form of a half cylinder on its side, There were two sets of four seats. Betty was placed in one of the seats that was shaped somewhat like an armchair. After flexible tubes had been placed into Betty's mouth and nostrils, a translucent canopy shaped like the seat was tilted down over Betty's body. After again being reassured telepathically, a grey liquid from tubes attached to the top of the chair filled the space between Betty and the canopy. She was fed with a spoonful of sweet, thick liquid, perhaps as a tranquillizer, and Betty began to feel vibrations. She felt a temporary heaviness, possibly the result of extreme acceleration. As the vibrations ceased, the grey liquid was drained from the chair and Betty emerged to see two of the creatures with black hoods over their heads.

With her clothes still wet from the liquid, Betty stepped out of the chair, and was manoeuvered into a standing position between the two creatures. As a threesome they were floated into a standing position onto a black track and they glided through a series of dark interconnecting tunnels. Betty's head and feet felt heavy as though her feet were glued into position. The only illumination was from the glowing silver suits worn by Betty's hooded companions. As they approached a silvery mirror-like material, Betty braced herself for the crash. Instead they passed through without incident into an atmosphere that was vibrating red, as though in a room bathed with infrared light. The track ran between two buildings with window-shaped openings. Climbing over the buildings were many thin monkey-like creatures, without tails and with gecko-like pad fingers. Instead of heads they had two stalks with a large eye atop each stalk. Each eye could swivel in any direction, The monkey-like creatures just stared as Betty and her companions glided past.

The trio then approached and passed through a circular membrane into a beautiful green atmosphere, with water enshrouded by mist on either side. As her companions removed their hoods, the one in front of Betty communicated telepathically to her, reminding her that he had told her not to be afraid. Betty found the plant life beautiful and yet so different from earth that she was unable to describe them. She saw a fishbird or birdfish that looks somewhat dolphin-like in one of the drawings made by Betty. She also saw buildings in the distance that looked like a city, although too far away for Betty to see any movement. The vast green area was criss-crossed with elevated walkways like bridges in the sky. Although there were domes in the distant city, the sky itself did not appear to be encased within a dome. Ahead of them Betty saw a series of variously shaped and sized crystals of stark beauty hanging in the sky, which sparkled brightly and gave off a beautiful rainbow effect.

After passing through the crystals, Betty saw an object in the distance in front of a bright light source. As they approached it became clear that the object was a giant 15-foot statue of an eagle with wings in the down position. They stepped off the black belt and Betty stood before the eagle. She experienced intense heat as if standing before a fire. She closed her eyes momentarily. When she opened them again, the eagle had been replaced by a small fire, which dimmed until the embers became grey ashes. To Betty's astonishment a thick grey worm emerged from the ashes. As the two entities stood to one side, Betty heard a booming voice saying to her, 'You have seen, and you have heard. Do you understand?' The voice called Betty's name again in a louder voice. Betty replied that she didn't know why she was there or what this was about. The voice replied, 'I have chosen you . . I have chosen you to show the world.' The voice was evasive in response to Betty's further questions about its identity. She asked if it was God or the Lord Jesus. When the voice spoke of her fear and told her to release herself from her fear 'through my son', Betty underwent a profound and moving religious experience.

At the end of the return journey back to earth, Quazgaa emerged from another part of the spacecraft to bid Betty farewell. He telepathically communicated a message to Betty similar to that given to many other abductees: about the dangers of mankind continuing on its present course – needing to learn love and about knowledge acquired through the spirit. Although much of Quazgaa's communication was enigmatic, his most surprising revelation was that many others have, like Betty, had secrets locked in their minds. When they returned Betty to her home in Massachusetts, one of the entities, who revealed his name as Joohop, spoke about the blue book that had been given to Betty. He referred to the writing as writing of light that can only be understood through the spirit. Man needs to understand nature, for he is also of nature. Love is the answer for man.

Betty was later subjected to a psychiatric examination as well as lie detector test to affirm the veracity of her story, and her freedom from psychosis or psychiatric disorder. When Betty was pressed by Ray Fowler and by Fred Youngren, who was also in attendance at the hypnotic regression sessions, about where she thought this world was located, she was clear that they had left our earth. She stated that they were both in space and yet in the centre of the earth, which Betty herself found puzzling. Further hypnotic regression sessions revealed that Betty had had a number of previous encounters at the ages of 7, 12, 13, 18 and 24. Considerable further detail about the aliens, their technology and their intentions are revealed by Ray Fowler in *The Andreasson Affair: Phase Two, The Watchers,* and *The Watchers II.*

Of all the subsequent revelations of Betty's experiences with the extraterrestrials, the one that provokes the greatest curiosity is the reason for the genetic reproduction and storage of human foetuses. This practice it seems is not limited to the more familiar greys. The most startling and sobering response to Betty's question to one of the aliens about the reason for their activities: 'We have to because as time goes by, mankind will become *sterile*. They will not be able to produce.' (Raymond Fowler, *The Watchers*).

Travis Walton, 1975, Herber, Arizona

Travis Walton's abduction took place on 15 November 1975 at a logging site near Herber, Arizona. He was aged 22 at the time, and a member of a six-man crew, all in their twenties, headed by Michael Rogers. They had been thinning and stacking timber in the Turkey Springs area of the Sitgreaves National Forest.

As Rogers described the incident in a tape-recorded interview three days later, the crew had finished work at dusk. They were driving along a rough logging road heading back to Snowflake, 45 miles away, via the village of Herber. Allan Dallis, who was sitting in the rear of the truck, was the first to see a yellowish glow through the heavy timber. When the truck reached a clearing, they saw a saucer-shaped object hovering less than 100 feet above a pile of cut timber. It was about 15 feet in diameter and 'looked like a flying saucer . . . something I'd seen pictures of'.

Walton yelled to Rogers to stop the truck; but before he could do so Walton opened the door, leapt out and walked towards the object. According to Walton, 'I got out of the truck and walked towards it. This may have been a foolish thing but I thought that it might just take off. I got out and tried to get a better look. This was not just a point of light in the sky . . . it was very close, you could have thrown a rock and hit it.'

The other five men watched as he approached the object. Suddenly he was struck by an intense blue-green light that resembled a lightning strike. The explosive force of this apparently defensive beam threw him back about 10 feet, seemingly unconscious.

In a panic, Mike Rogers gunned the truck and made a hasty exit. About a quarter of a mile down the road he regained his senses and realized that he had abandoned his friend and colleague. 'I turned the truck around and headed back . . . several of the men didn't want that at all . . . they were very afraid of what could happen to them if they went back to the site.'

At the site of the encounter there was no trace of Walton. 'The thing was gone. Travis was gone. It was a very traumatic experience, the most traumatic experience I've ever encountered. Something not of this world simply had taken Travis and he was just not there. What could we do? All we could think of was to go to the authorities.'

And so they did. Mike and the remainder of his crew contacted the sheriff in nearby Holbrook. He was cautious although not completely disbelieving. A large-scale manhunt was undertaken under his directions; but there was no sign of Walton, although there was a blackened slash at the spot where the men had seen him struck by the shaft from the alien craft.

The Sheriff began to suspect that the men had murdered Walton and buried his body in the woods; and that the UFO story was simply a ruse to cover the murder. The loggers were rigorously interrogated, and all agreed to take a lie-detector test in order to vindicate themselves.

The test was administered by C E Gilson. He had never previously conducted a test with so many participants describing one event. He was painstaking in his questioning in order to eliminate variations due to anxiety. His report stated: 'These polygraph examinations positively prove that these five men did see something they believe was a UFO and that Travis Walton was not injured or murdered by any of these men, on that Wednesday 5th of November 1975. If an actual UFO did not exist and the UFO was a man-made hoax, five of these men had no prior knowledge of a hoax.'

Five days passed before Walton finally returned. He telephoned his sister shortly after midnight, and spoke to her husband, Grant Neff. His voice sounded so befuddled, Neff later said, that he thought the caller was an intoxicated hoaxer. He was about to replace the telephone when Walton screamed his name and begged for help. He was calling from a payphone at a gas station near Herber. He was later found collapsed on the floor of the phone booth.

His body was subsequently found to have no bruises or burns, but there was a small red scab mark on the inside of his right elbow. Blood tests revealed no drugs in his body, but he had lost 10 pounds and was physically drained. Travis later told his remarkable story in *The Walton Experience*.

> When I felt the numbing shock, I blacked out. The next thing I remember was regaining consciousness. I was lying on my back on a table, my head was not very clear and I was in a lot of pain. The room I was in resembled a hospital and that's exactly where I thought I was.

He was terrified when he noticed two alien beings standing over him.

> These two things were standing there looking at me, these huge eyes just seemed to just look right through me. I didn't get much impression of emotion; just a kind of observing sort of emotion to them. They just stood there looking at me and damn those huge eyes! It looked very much like they knew exactly what I was thinking and feeling. These huge eyes were like a window opening and shutting . . . I just couldn't bear their gaze.

He grabbed a tubular-shaped object that was lying over his chest and adopted a defensive posture. The two aliens seemed to understand his emotions telepathically and left him alone, whereupon he ran down a hallway into a room where he saw what looked like a control console built into the arms of a chair.

> There was a lever there and when I moved it the star pattern in front of me moved. It was very disorienting because I saw this

pattern move and it felt like I was moving as well . . . I figured I better not play with that, feeling that I might crash this thing or something. I had by that time surmised that I was in some sort of craft and connected it with what happened earlier in the woods.

Another creature entered the room, who looked more human than the humanoids he had previously encountered.

This man was not like those humanoid things I saw earlier. This looked like a human being . . . like a man in a blue uniform. I went up to him thinking that I was being saved, that I was being rescued.

But the tall human-looking character was unresponsive when Walton spoke to him. He appeared not to understand what he was saying.

I could not get him to talk to me . . . it was clear he couldn't really understand what I was saying.

Walton ran out of the room, and continued down the hallway.

A door opened halfway down the hall and the air was very much fresher and easier to breathe than the air I was in. The air inside the craft was very heavy and moist . . . stifling.

He ran into yet another room, where he encountered two muscular, human-looking figures, who quickly detained him. They propped him into an unusual chair that looked like an examination chair, after which he could remember nothing until he awoke five days later in the countryside.

The thing that has brought more frustration into my life as a result of all of this happening is the fact that people don't see me anymore, me as a person. I get this feeling of invisibility because of this thing. Every contact I have with people is filtered through the distorting lens of something that just happened to me 15 years ago. I'm not a deceiving liar or crackpot space cadet sort of person. This just happened to me; it could have happened to anyone!

The remarkable features of the Travis Walton case were his physical scars and the witnesses who saw the spacecraft.

Abductions around the world

Although the above four cases all took place in the USA, abductions are a worldwide phenomenon. The impression that more abductions take place in the USA than elsewhere is probably the result of more effective co-ordination of reports via the regional structure of the numerous UFO research organizations, and a greater readiness to talk about unusual experiences than in the more traditional societies.

But extraterrestrial contact, although not necessarily abduction, is known to indigenous native Americans. The Cherokee and the Hopi refer to these beings as 'star people'. In South Africa, a leading sangoma, or medicine man, calls them 'mandingdas'. And the religious beliefs of the Dogon people who live in the Homburi Mountains near Timbuktu, Mali, are based on their knowledge of the Sirius B star system. Their knowledge was obtained before Western astronomers even had a photograph of the star. They claim to have received their extraordinarily detailed information from visitors from another star system.

EVIDENCE OF ABDUCTIONS

Physical marks

The physical marks on people's bodies are the most consistent supporting evidence of their abduction. The most common scar is usually referred to as a 'scoop mark' – a small round depression, slightly smaller than a thumbnail: $1/8$–$3/4$ inch in diameter and as much as $1/4$ inch deep. It looks as if a tool has neatly removed a layer of cells. The scars seldom vary in appearance, and appear on different parts of the body. Another typical scar is a straight thin surgical cut – between 1 and 3 inches long; also found on different parts of the body. There is rarely any bleeding after the abduction.

Large bruises are often visible the next morning on the insides of the thighs of women abductees, often accompanied by dramatic-looking scars. In one case a doctor consulted by an abductee firmly believed that she had had surgery because of small extensions along one of the cuts.

The presence of UFOs

The lack of independent evidence to corroborate the stories of abductees continues to provide fuel for the sceptics. But in some cases UFOs have been observed, and filmed on camera, at the same time that people have been abducted. The most dramatic case is the story of Linda Napolitano, who claims to have been abducted in November 1989 from a high-rise Manhattan apartment block. A number of people, including two police officers, saw a woman float out of an apartment window towards a hovering UFO. The policemen were ferrying a prominent politician to a nearby heliport when their car stalled. The politician, whose identity remains unknown, also observed the event. And in the case of Travis Walton, his colleagues observed the craft before he was beamed up.

UFOs have in fact often been reported by the local community and the media at the same time that abductees have said they were removed. William Herrmann of Charleston, South Carolina, actually saw the alien spacecraft prior to being abducted in March 1978.

The evidence of witnesses

Betty Andreasson's father saw a group of aliens making their way towards the house from an adjacent field: 'These creatures I saw through the window of Betty's house were just like Halloween freaks. I thought they had put on a funny kind of headdress imitating a moon man.'

People have also been observed to be missing at the time they say their abduction took place, although this is not very well documented. There have also been cases in which the bodies of abductees have been seen at the same that they were ostensibly abducted. In *The Complete Book of UFOs*, Jenny Randles and Peter Hough refer to a case in Australia in which

> ... a woman had an encounter with a UFO and entities. Two witnesses who were with her at the time saw her interacting with these beings and then 'enter' the UFO as if abducted by it. However, she [her body] never physically went anywhere. She remained in their view seemingly talking to thin air, encountering an object that neither of them could see and which, by standard definitions of reality, was not actually there.

This paradoxical example certainly lends fuel to those who argue that abductions are not actual physical events, but either spiritual/shamanic journeys taking place in another dimension or fantasies taking place in the minds of the abductees. Randles and Hough do not, however, provide any further details of the event they describe – no date, no names. It is therefore not particularly strong evidence either for or against the tangible nature of abductions.

The case of Linda Napolitano, who was seen floating out of the window of her Manhattan apartment block, is also not conclusive on this specific point – nobody actually saw that her physical body was not in her apartment.

But the principal evidence to support the veracity of abduction accounts is the continuing consistency between reports. Time and again people who are completely unknown to each other report similar experiences.

INSIDE A UFO

Have you ever wondered what an alien craft might look like inside? If the information collected by Temple University historian David Jacobs is correct, it may now be possible to know. After interviewing 50 UFO abductees who say they have been taken some 275 times, Jacobs has pieced together a picture of what is 'under the dome'.

The information is incomplete, says Jacobs, because the atmosphere aboard a UFO is businesslike, and no one is offered a guided tour. Abductees are there for a physical examination, he says, and they only see as much of the craft as is necessary for that purpose. That is why they invariably describe Spartan, efficient and sterile surroundings, with virtually no luxury features at all. The rooms are clinical-looking, with domed ceilings, skylight-like windows and grey or white walls. And the aliens are good housekeepers. 'It is clean and neat,' Jacobs says. 'We have had some cases where people vomited and it was cleaned up immediately.'

Despite these broad similarities, he adds, there are at least two types of craft, 'with the typical large UFO checking in at about 200 feet in diameter and its smaller cousin at about 35 feet. If the craft is on the ground, abductees climb a staircase that is lowered from the object. But if the vessel is hovering, they are floated up.' They find themselves in a hallway with metallic walls that are usually bare but sometimes contain a floor-to-ceiling window. Usually they are ushered along a curved corridor, which gives them the feeling that they are walking around the perimeter of the ship, although no one makes a complete circuit. Eventually they are led to the vessel's centre, the 'medical arena', where unpleasant physical examinations occur.

Virtually all medical zones are illuminated by a mysterious light source that abductees cannot locate, Jacobs says. But they have pinpointed the position of voluminous medical equipment – attached to walls and ceilings, in drawers, or on rolling carts. As for the examination table, Jacobs says, it is generally 'hard with very little give', and contains lighted, arm-like devices snaking up from its sides.

In many cases, the examination room resembles the hub of a wheel. The spokes, or hallways, lead from there to other chambers, which are revealed only to some abductees after the examination. These chambers are also circular, with domed ceilings, white or grey walls, and built-in benches. Some seem to be 'visiting rooms' in which human-alien hybrid babies are touched, held or viewed.

Finally, abductees may pass through a control room containing a console with lights, an unpadded seat, and no windows.

While all this detail is fascinating, equally interesting according to Jacobs is what abductees do not report. His witnesses are remarkably consistent in being unable to describe the living areas. 'Of course', he says, 'that doesn't mean they don't exist in other parts of the UFO.'

THE PHYSICAL APPEARANCE OF THE ALIENS

Although Lyssa Royal identifies fourteen different types of alien visitors in her channelling sessions, abductees have only described the beings known as 'greys'. They seem to come in four configurations. The shortest are between 3 and 4 feet tall. They wear no body suits and display no genital organs, although their gender can be sensed. They are mind-probers. They show little desire to communicate with abductees, and seem to float rather than walk.

The greys who play the role of biological technicians are slightly taller, between 4 and 5 feet in height. They behave with less indifference towards abductees and manifest a degree of feelings. It is uncertain whether this type is related to the shorter greys, or whether they are a taller version of the same species.

The third type is about 6 feet tall, with yellow, wig-like hair, and a dark grey body suit. They fly the cigar-shaped craft, and are therefore probably specialist pilots or navigators. They are rumoured to be able to change their form to that of an animal or a 'light-being'. Some abductees refer to this type as the Nordics, and they believe that they are unrelated to the little greys.

The tallest greys are over 7 feet tall. They look and walk like praying mantises, and behave as if they are the diplomats. This could be the type referred to as the Reptilians.

The first two types described above compare only vaguely with those described in the MJ-12 Special Operations Manual of April 1954 (*see* chapter 3). There, EBE Type II is described as bluish-grey in colour, between 3 feet 5 inches and 4 feet 2 inches in height, with slanted, wrap-around eyes and a ridge running over the crown of the head. This latter characteristic has not to my knowledge been described by any abductees. MJ-12's EBE Type I is described as having a chalky-white colour and an Oriental appearance with small wide-set almond-shaped eyes and as being between 5 feet and 5 feet 4 inches in height.

According to Michelle LaVigne the little people are mostly ashen in colour, although she has seen aliens whose skin tone is pale blue and others who are white, yellow and golden. Some abductees report little 'greys' who are bright purple and even red.

ABDUCTION AS A PHYSICAL OR SPIRITUAL PHENOMENON

Given our 'either/or' mentality, many people have difficulty embracing the idea that these creatures may be both physical and spiritual, and to have developed greater mastery over their spirit-being than we have, which may account for their ability to walk through walls and communicate telepathically. Our tendency to focus exclusively on physical reality results in most spirit experiences being relegated to the ranks of the unusual and the paranormal. Cases have been reported of abductees' spirit bodies being enticed out of their physical bodies, and of persons being able to look back and see the physical body still lying in bed, but these out-of-body experiences (OBEs) are not common. And although most abductions take place covertly, and witnesses are usually put in a state of paralysis, there is some, albeit scarce, evidence of the abductee's physical body being absent during an abduction.

Dr Kenneth Ring, Professor of Psychology at the University of Connecticut at Storrs, who is a specialist in OBEs and near death experiences (NDEs), advances the view that abductions are spiritual experiences which take place in another dimension:

> We could be in the beginning stages of a major shift in *levels of consciousness* that will eventually lead to humanity's being able to live in *two* worlds at once – the physical and the imaginal. (*The Omega Project*, p240)

He suggests that abductions are akin to a shamanic journey, implying that we have, in a sense, two bodies, one physical and one spirit or ethereal, and that actions performed in the spirit body are reflected by the physical body. Although he does not specifically say so, the implication is that extra-terrestrials are able to separate the spirit body from the physical body and remove it to another place. The physical body is left behind in a comatose state or an altered state of consciousness. The experiments then performed on the spirit or ethereal body are manifested in the physical body, to which the spirit body is later returned.

From this viewpoint, the physical body is seen as a shadow of the spirit body, a view that has been stated throughout the ages by various highly spiritual people, a view that is often lost in our materially oriented culture, which tends to validate only the physical and the tangible. Consequently, most of us remain strongly rooted in our physical body with scant sense of the potential of the spirit or ethereal element of our being.

Perhaps the greys are more evolved than humans and have developed greater control over their spirit bodies. This could account for their reputed ability to walk through solid objects, as reported by many abductees. This would suggest that the visitors have either discovered the secrets of separating the ethereal body from the physical body or that the abduction is a spiritual event. The visitors have been seen by witnesses other than the abductees themselves floating thorough doors and walls, while many abductees report being floated out of their bedrooms through closed windows.

Abductees regularly report hearing the voices of their abductors in their minds as in a telepathic communication. Many describe the voices as being like a raspy whisper.

Antonio Villas Boas (*see* p59) described hearing the aliens speaking among themselves in dog-like barks, although the sound that they make when speaking to each is more typically described by other abductees as a series of chirps. Michelle LaVigne writes that her friends chirp like squirrels when they laugh. She describes their speech as nasal, pronouncing their words with a mechanical tone.

On the other hand, the evidence, albeit circumstantial, is that the greys are real in a very physical sense. It must, however, be said that although this evidence might survive in a court case which depends 'on the balance of probability', it would not succeed in a case where proof is required to be 'beyond a reasonable doubt.' 'I suggest that the jury is still out on this case!

One of the strongest arguments for the physical nature of abductions is that the greys appear to be using human genetic material to create a race of hybrids for an as yet unknown purpose. In order to accomplish this purpose they surreptitiously remove physical human bodies from their beds and other places for varying periods of time.

THE ABDUCTEES

Their psychological state

There is no indication that abductees suffer from any specific psychopathological dysfunction. In a study of nine abductees conducted by Ted Bloecher, Budd Hopkins and Dr Aphrodite Clamar in 1981, there were five men and four women – a college lecturer, an electronics expert, an actor/tennis instructor, a corporation lawyer, a commercial artist, a business executive, a research chemist, a salesman/audio technician and a secretary.

Dr Elizabeth Slater, who conducted the evaluation without knowing that they were abductees, found them to be a diverse group, but with certain common characteristics. She described them as anxious, suffering from low self-esteem, wary, cautious, oversensitive and vulnerable to insults – but not paranoid or psychotic in any way. She was very surprised when she was told that the subjects were abductees because of their lack of psychological disorders – a point on which she was specific.

Abductions take place regardless of whether the abductees are awake and conscious or sleeping, but as far as we know, they do not remain asleep. Time and again abductees insist that their experience is real and not a dream or hallucination. Some recall very specifically being touched on the forehead by a device that looks like a car aerial. And the scars on their bodies bear testimony to the physical reality of the experience.

Abductees often speak of their world-view being shattered

by their experiences. Because of the unusual nature of an alien abduction, they question their own sanity – not usually the sign of a mentally unstable person. The experience is invariably very frightening until they come to terms with its reality.

Commentators who refer to abductees as mad or halluci-nating appear to be doing them a grave disservice and perpetuating their trauma. To be told that the experience is not real, but simply an hallucination, is like being mugged or raped twice – the second time for having the temerity to report the first assault.

Abduction as a psychosocial phenomenon

The ability of some people to create physical bodily symptoms, such as those who identify with the suffering of Christ by exhibiting stigmata, shows the power of the mind to affect the body. But the random distribution of cuts, bruises and lesions on the bodies of abductees tends to argue against abductions as similar psychosocial phenomena.

Carl Jung has frequently been quoted as one of the strongest proponents of the theory that UFOs are a psychosocial phenomenon and a product of our collective unconscious. But those who cite him in order to invalidate abduction reports, are not telling the whole story, because Jung believed that 'UFOs cannot be disposed of in this simple manner'. He also presents a problem for those who quote him in support of the argument that UFO sightings take place entirely in the minds of observers because of the lack of clarity that pervades almost all of his writing. This is amply demonstrated in *Flying Saucers: a Modern Myth*, in which Jung writes:

> It remains an established fact, supported by numerous obser-vations, that UFOs have not only been seen visually but have also been picked up on radar screens and have left traces on the photographic plate . . . It boils down to nothing less than this: that either psychic projections throw back a radar echo, or else the appearance of real objects affords an opportunity for mythological projections.

He clearly acknowledged the physical reality of UFOs on our planet. It should also be noted that his observations preceded the multiple reports of abductions.

The social and professional consequences of reporting an abduction

Many professionals fail to report abductions for fear of the consequences for their career. Sightings of objects create controversy enough; abductions are considerably more personal and intrusive. And people who report either experience are known to have created problems for themselves.

Many airline pilots have been grounded after reporting a sighting of a UFO, and therefore they tend not to say anything. A recent survey has revealed that some 25–30 per cent of airline pilots have had close-up sightings of alien spacecraft, but few have reported them. The notable exception was the Japanese crew of flight JAL 1628.

In the early hours of 17 November 1986, a cargo flight with a crew of three was on its way from Paris via Reykjavik and Anchorage to Tokyo. Captain Kenju Terauchi's dialogue with Anchorage Air Route Traffic Control Center (AARTCC), which lasted 34 minutes and 16 seconds, was recorded. After some conversation, AARTCC told Captain Terauchi that he was not alone in the sky above Alaska: 'JAL1628 Heavy. Military radar advises they are picking up intermittent primary target behind you in trail, in trail, I say again.' Such independent confirmation, however, is rare.

Although the climate of opinion is changing, academics and scientists still tend to be fearful of damage to their credibility and consequent loss of preferment and funding if they talk openly about alien abductions. The subject is still largely taboo. The fact that so many people are willing to suffer the risks to their social acceptability, career advancement and financial security, bears testimony to the strength of their belief in what they are saying.

Memory block and immobilization of witnesses

The inability of many abductees to recall their experience suggests that they have been specifically told by their abductors that they will not remember the event. Many people imagine that amnesia is a by-product of hypnosis because television hypnotists often tell their subjects to forget what took place while they were hypnotized. But the purpose of hypnosis therapy is the precise opposite – to enable the client to recall an experience that has been buried in the unconscious, where it is causing a disturbance.

Regression therapy is a standard psychotherapeutic technique in which the client is taken back to the disturbing event. They then have an opportunity to relive and re-experience the emotions surrounding the event, thus removing the trauma and the emotional sting from the memory. Regression hypnosis enables the barrier imposed by the alien to be breached. In fact many abductees recall, during subsequent regression therapy sessions, that they were told by their abductors to forget their visit to the alien craft and the examination performed on them.

In a similar way, witnesses are generally put into a dormant state and are unaware of the abduction. By the time they are brought back to full awareness the abductee has been returned. Linda Napolitano described her terror at noticing that her two young children had been rendered unconscious by her abductors.

THE EXAMINATION

There is some evidence, although it is still inconclusive, of implants being put into human bodies. Small round balls the size of mustard seeds have been found in the nasal passages of some abductees. Thin pieces of metal the size of a small nail have also been seen in X-rays of the feet of others.

The usual descriptions of examinations, however, are of complex processes whereby sperm is removed from the men and ova from the women. Michelle LaVigne, in her book *The Alien Abduction Survival Guide*, refers to men being 'placed on a table and a tube, which comes from the wall, is placed over the penis . . . and the sperm is forcibly collected'. She describes women having their legs guided apart and their feet put in stirrups as a 'tube that comes out of the wall is inserted into her body vaginally and eggs are taken from her'.

Genetic material is inserted into a woman's uterus vaginally, and the foetal implant is removed two or three months later by 'phasing', a process whereby one object is moved through another. The foetus is therefore removed through the woman's body with the placenta intact rather than through the vagina. Women are used many times to breed foetuses for the first few months before they are removed for further development. According to Hetar, Michelle LaVigne's diminutive grey 'guide', she has been used in this way to create hybrids no less than 63 times.

In Raymond Fowler's *The Watchers*, Betty Andreasson is reported as seeing aliens 'working near [another] woman's legs . . . removing a very small, strange-looking fetus'. She also described the eyebrows of the foetus being cut and the foetus placed in a translucent jar with tubes attached, like an artificial womb, where it was presumably brought to term. Another abductee provides the following description of a bank of foetuses:

> The long wall that was over on my left, receded up into the ceiling. And it revealed row upon row upon row of canisters. I don't know if they were made out of glass, plexiglass, plastic – I don't know. Canisters. They were filled with a clear luminous green liquid and inside each canister, attached by little wires and things, was one of these little hybrids. It was just suspended in there.

Other abductees state that it is the intention of the greys to populate the world with their hybrids once the human race completes its destruction of the earth as a living system. Michelle LaVigne concludes that it is the intention of the greys to replace humans with the hybrids by a concerted programme of cross-breeding – and that this programme has already begun.

I was myself surprised by a seven-year-old boy whom I met with his parents in Colorado, who quite unabashedly claimed to be an alien life form from another planet, who chose to live on earth. The extraordinary part of his communication was the blend of mature adult and child in the way that he communicated – and with a knowledge of information which was by all accounts not provided him by his parents.

I have subsequently had reports of at least two other boys of similar age, all born in 1990. All communicate in a similar manner and manifest a certain maturity of attitude not usually associated with children in that age group. All three boys speak of their other home on another planet. In one case where such talk is discouraged by one of the grandparents, the boy tends, not unnaturally, to speak less about his 'other life'.

Could these boys be a sign of hybrid beings who have a completely human body, but with a level of awareness that is beyond this world? Could there be more children who tell a similar story, the significance of which is unrecognized because they are dismissed as childish fantasies?

Richard and Lee Boylan write in *Close Extraterrestrial Encounters* about women who give birth to and rear 'a human-appearing child with exceptional intelligence, cosmic aware-ness, and/or psychic powers'. Their conclusion is that extraterrestrials are 'engaging in genetic engineering and/or partial hybridization to gradually enhance the overall abilities of the human race and provide leaders with superior abilities during the predicted difficult transition times ahead. My [Richard Boylan's] research seems to support this hypothesis.'

WHAT IS THE PURPOSE BEHIND THESE ENCOUNTERS?

This question is the subject of endless speculation, resulting in few answers. According to the Roper Organization, there were an average of more than 3,000 abductions or other CE4s per day in the USA alone in 1992. If this is the case, the greys appear to be conducting a massive breeding programme. It is unclear whether their intention is to remove the hybrids to their planet, or whether they intend to introduce them into our society.

Some researchers have speculated that the greys are suffering from a genetic disorder and are unable to replicate themselves.

UFO Museum and Research Center, Roswell.

Crashed saucer display at the UFO Enigma Museum, Roswell.

Roswell air base where dead aliens were allegedly stored.

Display portraying alien autopsy at UFO museum in Roswell.

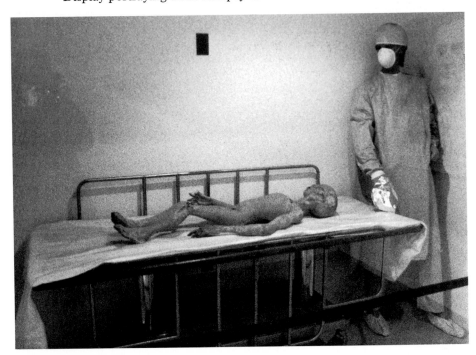

Brigadier General Roger R Ramey, commander of the Eighth Air Force, and Major Jesse Marcel, intelligence officer at Roswell AAF, pictured with material from the crashed 'flying disk'. Marcel claimed that Ramey switched the real wreckage for that of a weather balloon.

The Roswell story unfolds on the front pages of the July 8 (above) and 9 (right) issues of *Roswell Daily Record*.

RAAF Captures Flying Saucer On Ranch in Roswell Region

No Details of Flying Disk Are Revealed

Roswell Hardware Man and Wife Report Disk Seen

The intelligence office of the 509th Bombardment group at Roswell Army Air Field announced at noon today, that the field has come into possession of a flying saucer.

According to information released by the department, over authority of Maj. J. A. Marcel, intelligence officer, the disk was recovered on a ranch in the Roswell vicinity, after an unidentified rancher had notified Sheriff Geo. Wilcox, here, that he had found the instrument on his premises.

Major Marcel and a detail from his department went to the ranch and recovered the disk, it was stated.

After the intelligence office here had inspected the instrument it was flown to "higher headquarters."

The intelligence office stated that no details of the saucer's construction or its appearance had been revealed.

Mr. and Mrs. Dan Wilmot apparently were the only persons in Roswell who have seen what they thought was a flying disk.

They were sitting on their porch at 105 South Penn. last Wednesday night at about ten minutes before ten o'clock when a large glowing object zoomed out of the sky from the southeast, going in a northwesterly direction at a high rate of speed.

Wilmot called Mrs. Wilmot's attention to it and both ran down into the yard to watch. It was in sight less than a minute, perhaps 40 or 50 seconds, Wilmot estimated.

Wilmot said that it appeared to him to be about 1,500 feet high and going fast. He estimated between 400 and 500 miles per hour.

In appearance it looked oval in shape like two inverted saucers, faced mouth to mouth, or like two old type washbowls placed together in the same fashion. The entire body glowed as though light were showing through from inside, though not like it would be if a light were merely underneath.

From where he stood Wilmot said that the object looked to be about 5 feet in size, and making allowance for the distance it was from town he figured that it must have been 15 or 20 feet in diameter, though this was just a guess.

Wilmot said that he heard no sound but that Mrs. Wilmot said she heard a swishing sound for a very short time.

The object came into view from the southeast and disappeared over the treetops in the general vicinity of six-mile hill.

Wilmot, who is one of the most respected and reliable citizens in town, kept the story to himself hoping that someone else would come out and tell about having seen one, but finally today decided that he would go ahead and tell about seeing it. The announcement that the RAAF was in possession of one came only a few minutes after he had decided to release the details of what he had seen.

―――o―――

Air Force General Says Army Not Doing Experiments

Portland. Ore., July 8 (AP)—The Oregonian said today that Maj. Gen. Nathan F. Twining, chief of the AAF material command. told it flatly that the "flying saucers" are not the result of experiments by the armed services.

"Neither the AAF nor any other component of the armed forces had any plane, guided missile or other aerial device under development which could possibly be mistaken for a saucer or formation of flying discs," the newspaper quoted Twining as telling it by telephone from Kirtland Army Airbase. Albuquerque. N. M.

It continued its quotation: "Some of these witnesses evidently saw something but we don't know what we are investigating."

Meanwhile, air National Guard squadrons flying from Portland. Boise and Spokane bases patrolled Pacific Northwest skies late yesterday, landing after sundown, without observing any of the objects.

Col. G. Robert Doddson, commanding the 123rd and 116th squadrons, said camera-equipped planes would take the air twice daily from the three fields.

―――o―――

LA DOMENICA DEL CORRIERE

Supplemento settimanale illustrato del nuovo CORRIERE DELLA SERA - Abbonamenti: Italia, anno L. 1400, sem. L. 750 - Estero, anno L. 2000, sem. L. 1050

Anno 56 — N. 40   3 Ottobre 1954   L. 30.–

Che cosa era? Sul cielo di Roma è apparso sere fa uno strano corpo rossiccio dalla forma di mezzo sigaro, che lasciava dietro di sé una scia fumosa. Viaggiava a velocità ridotta e a non più di 1300 metri di quota. L'hanno visto migliaia di cittadini, l'hanno avvistato le stazioni dell'aeroporto di Ciampino, l'ha intercettato il radar dell'aeroporto di Pratica di Mare. Il radar ha anche accertato che la "cosa,, misteriosa aveva un'antenna sporgente nel punto della massima circonferenza. I competenti escludono che possa trattarsi di un meteorite. (Disegno di Walter Molino)

In the years following the Roswell incident, reports of UFO sightings came in from around the world. This one, described in *La Domenica del Corriere* on 4 October 1954, comes from Italy. The caption translates as:

What was it? Last evening a strange reddish 'body' in the shape of a half cigar appeared in the sky above Rome, leaving behind it a trail of smoke. It travelled at a frightening speed and was not more than 1300 metres above the ground. Thousands of inhabitants saw it, Ciampino airport was warned of it, the airport at Practica de Mare intercepted it with its radar. The radar ascertained that the mysterious 'thing' had an antenna sprouting from its point of maximum circumference. Those qualified to judge declared that it could not possibly have originated from a meteorite.

Stanton Friedman holding pages of the Majestic-12 special operations manual, *Extraterrestrial Entities and Technology, Recovery and Disposal*. This document first came to light in December 1994 when Don Berliner received a roll of film through the post containing photographs of 18 pages. Friedman evaluates the authenticity of the document in his book, *Top Secret/Majic*.

UFO from Coma Berenices, at Peralta, New Mexico,
photographed by Paul Villa.

Experimental disk constructed to specifications provided by aliens,
photographed by Paul Villa.

During the 1970s, Eduard 'Billy' Meier from Switzerland claimed contact with beings from the Pleiades and photographed their craft.

Highway patrol officer Lonnie Zamora, who saw a UFO at Socorro, New Mexico on 24 April 1964.

Indentation (protected by stones) left by the UFO seen by Lonnie Zamora.

(*above*) Chris Lambright's painting of the spacecraft, with insignia as described to him by Lonnie Zamora – an egg-shaped craft on four thin legs; (*below*) drawings by Chris Lambright from which Lonnie Zamora ticked the shape closest to that of the craft he saw.

Which shape is closest to
the object you saw?

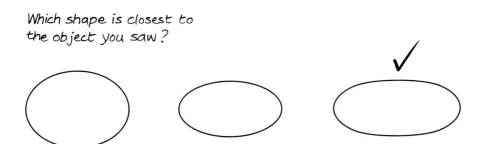

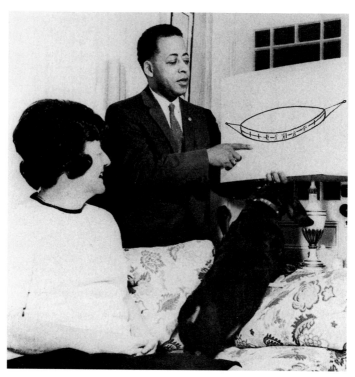

(*above*) Betty and Barney Hill who, under regression therapy, described being abducted in September 1961 in Portsmouth, New Hampshire. Barney Hill is holding a drawing of the craft into which they claim they were taken. Whilst on board, Betty asked the leader of the aliens where they came from. In reply he showed her a star map which she was able to sketch later (*below*). This is said to represent the star system Zeta Reticuli.

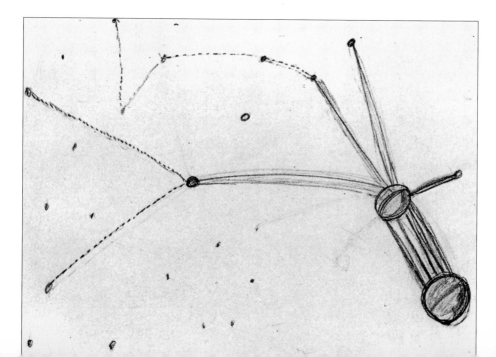

(*left*) Travis Walton, who was abducted in Arizona on 15 November 1975. In the presence of five witnesses, he was knocked unconscious by an intense beam of light from a hovering space-ship.

(*below*) While his companions drove off in panic, he was abducted and was not seen again for five days.

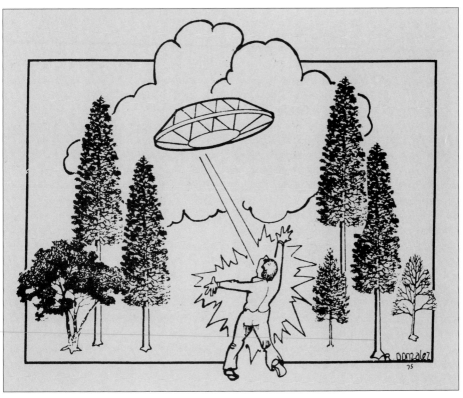

Betty Andreasson, who was abducted from her home in Ashburnham, Massachusetts on 25 January 1967. Her outlandish experiences were uncovered during a series of hypnotic regressions. At one point in her journey she encountered a 15-foot high statue of an eagle. As she stood in front of it, the statue burnt to ashes from which a gray, claylike worm emerged (*opposite*).

I stood about this tall before it.

It looked like a 15-foot eagle, but its neck was longer. It spread its wings, shielding the light behind it.

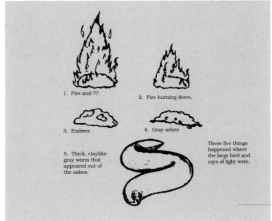

1. Fire and ??

2. Fire burning down.

3. Embers

4. Gray ashes

5. Thick, claylike gray worm that appeared out of the ashes.

These five things happened where the large bird and rays of light were.

Lyssa Royal is one of the most prominent channellers, channelling three different extraterrestrial entities: Sasha is a female from the Pleiades star group; Bashar is a male Essassani – a genetic cross between humans and beings from Zeta Reticuli; Germane is a non-physical group consciousness which provides much information about extraterrestrial history.

This sounds unlikely in a group of very clever people who are able to travel many light years and several other dimensions in order to visit us; but the theory deserves some consideration in view of their extended human breeding programme, in which some of their own qualities are being bred into the hybrids in order to perpetuate their own line.

However the greys are biological entities, not warm-blooded mammals who need to consume other animals to survive. Judging by the way that their craft fly, their bodies are able to withstand forces of 40g as their craft weave and jink across our skies, whereas humans, who are 70 per cent water, cannot survive more than 7g without blacking out. Mixing a race of primitive, disease-ridden, warm-blooded mammals with a race of biological entities sounds worse than trying to mix a mule with a thoroughbred. The most remarkable feature of human beings from an extraterrestrial perspective, I would suggest, is our ability to breed prolifically, no matter what the circumstances.

Conversely, given the superiority of the greys, it would make more sense viewed from their perspective to create a race of hybrids in order to introduce their qualities into the human race, rather than to introduce our qualities into their race. In a nutshell: are the hybrids being created so that we can save the greys or so that the greys can save us?

The 'grand human disaster scenario' is that the greys plan for the hybrids to become teachers and caretakers to lead us out of the darkness and chaos created by pollution and natural disasters. Their intention is to assist us to develop our dormant spiritual and psychic abilities, and thereby enable us to become members of the intergalactic federation.

Seth, who has been channelled by Jane Roberts, describes his mission as being 'to bridge the gap between human and extraterrestrial communication and to establish the potential for technological exchange and interplanetary trade'. Sasha, on the other hand, who is channelled by Lyssa Royal, provides a wealth of information about the mechanics of extraterrestrial contact but no specific reason for the alien visitors, other than their desire for us to become part of an 'association of worlds,' whether we like it or not. They have decided that our time has come to emerge, and that as quasi-parents, it has fallen to them to draw us into this wider community. According to Sasha, we have misunderstood the role of the Zeta Reticuli, the greys, because we have assigned them a parental role and view them through a distorted reality screen.

The consistent message, which comes across continuously, is the aliens' concern about the physical state of the world. The earth is in serious trouble while we, as a race, have suicidal tendencies. They believe that we are heading into oblivion without care or concern. They are interceding in order to protect the earth, and possibly ourselves, from our worst ravages. They have assigned themselves the role of caretakers.

HAVE YOU HAD AN ALIEN ENCOUNTER?

Millions of people have had encounters with alien beings without realizing it. Alien abductors appear to be highly skilled at suppressing the memories of their abductees, which often remain deeply buried and can cause confusion or an unexplained feeling of unease.

After a detailed analysis of the common symptoms that characterize abductions, Melinda Leslie and Mark Williams have compiled a list of 52 questions showing common indicators of an abduction. The purpose is to help people determine whether they or someone they know is an abductee. To establish how likely it is that you are an abductee, consider carefully the questions, in any sequence, and make a note of your responses.

1 Have you experienced missing or lost time, especially an hour or more?
2 Have you felt paralysed in bed while you have a sense of another being in the room?
3 Do you have unusual scars or marks with no possible explanation of how you received them – a small scoop indentation, a straight line scar, scars in the roof of your mouth, in your nose, behind or in your ears or in the genital area? – and had an emotional reaction to them?

4 Have you seen balls or flashes of light in your home or elsewhere?

5 Do you have a memory of flying through the air?

6 Do you have a 'marker memory' that will not go away – an alien face, an examination, a needle, a table, a strange baby?

7 Have you seen beams of light outside your home, or shining through your bedroom window?

8 Have you had dreams of UFOs, beams of light or alien beings?

9 Have you ever seen a UFO or strange objects?

10 Do you have a cosmic awareness or an interest in ecology, the environment or vegetarianism, or are you very socially conscious?

11 Do you have a strong sense of having a mission or important task to perform, without knowing where this compulsion comes from?

12 Have events ever taken in place in your life about which you felt strangely anxious afterwards?

13 If you are a woman, have you suffered from a false pregnancy or had a foetus go mysteriously missing?

14 Have you woken in a place other than where you went to sleep?

15 Do you often dream of animal eyes – typically those of an owl or deer – or remember seeing an animal looking in at you, and do you have a fear of eyes?

16 Have you often woken with a start in the middle of the night?

17 Do you have a strong reaction to pictures of aliens – either drawn towards them or repelled by them?

18 Do you have inexplicably strong fears of heights, snakes, spiders, large insects, certain sounds, bright lights or of being alone?

19 Do you suffer from low self-esteem?

20 Have you observed a sleeping partner become paralysed, motionless or frozen in time?

21 Have you woken with burns or bruises which appeared during the night with no indication of how you have received them?

22 Has anyone claimed to have witnessed a UFO or an alien presence in your area around the time that you have had a missing or lost time experience?

23 Have you found blood or an inexplicable stain on your pillow or on a sheet?

24 Do you find that you have either a compulsion for, or an aversion to, UFOs and the subject of extraterrestrials?

25 Have you experienced a sudden compulsion to drive or walk to a remote location, or to a place completely unknown to you?

26 Do you feel that you are being watched, especially at night?

27 Have you ever had dreams about passing through a closed window or a solid wall?

28 Have you ever observed a strange fog or haze that seemed unusual?

29 Have you ever heard strange humming or pulsing sounds from an unidentifiable source?

30 Have you woken with a nosebleed, or experienced a nosebleed for no apparent reason?

31 Have you woken with a genital pain without an identifiable cause?

32 Have you woken with an abnormal stiffness in the body, particularly the T-3 vertebra area?

33 Do you suffer from chronic sinusitis or nasal problems?

34 Have you noticed electrical and electronic devices malfunctioning in your presence, typically street lights as you walk past them, and radio and TVs as you move close to them?

35 Do you recall seeing a hooded figure in or near your home, especially next to your bed?

36 Do you hear a frequent or sporadic ringing in your ears, especially in just one ear?

37 Do you have an abnormal fear of doctors or tend to avoid medical treatment beyond what would seem reasonable?

38 Are you suffering from insomnia in a way that seems strange to you?

39 Do you have dreams or nightmares of doctors and medical procedures?

40 Do you suffer from frequent headaches, especially in the sinus, behind one eye, or in one ear?

41 Did you feel that you were going crazy for considering the subject of the questions in this survey, before reading this list?

42 Have you had numerous paranormal or psychic experiences?

43 Are you prone to compulsive or addictive behaviour?

44 Have you channelled telepathic messages from extra-terrestrial sources?

45 Are you afraid of your wardrobe, or have you been in the past?

46 Have you had a mysterious feeling that you must not become involved in a relationship because it would interfere with something important you must accomplish?

47 Do you find it absolutely essential that you sleep with your bed against a wall?

48 Do you find it difficult to trust other people, especially authority figures?

49 Are your dreams about destruction or catastrophe?

50 Do you feel that you are deeply inhibited from talking about the questions raised in this list?

51 Have you tried in the past to resolve a number of the issues listed in this questionnaire?

52 Are many of your answers positive even though you have no conscious recollection of an abduction or alien encounter?

If you have answered positively to a significant number of these questions, you *may* have been abducted – *but please note that this is not an absolute indication.* You should regard with caution any conclusion that you may come to. Many of the questions could of course relate to experiences that are unconnected with abductions, and others could refer to psychic experiences unaffected by alien interference. The significance of the test is in the total number of positive answers that you score.

These questions have not been weighted in any way, and it is therefore difficult to say how many positive answers would indicate a possible abduction experience. My estimate for the following number of positive answers would be roughly as follows:

1–10 suggests that it is unlikely that you have been abducted.

11–20 gives some cause for concern, but insufficient to suggest an abduction.

21–30 is significant and may well indicate one or more abductions.

31–40 suggests a significant possibility that you have been abducted.

41–52 would suggest either that you have cheated or that you need immediate assistance.

I would recommend that you seek the help of a qualified researcher or therapist with experience of regression therapy – one who will provide you with the opportunity to explore your experience with an open mind, and who is not mainly concerned to prove that your experience is an hallucination.

5

GOVERNMENT INVOLVEMENT AND COVER-UP

The US government successfully debunked and buried any evidence that an alien spacecraft had crashed near Roswell in 1947. It took more than 30 years for the truth to emerge, which it finally did mainly due to the painstaking efforts of Stanton Friedman, Kevin Randle, Don Schmitt and others. Stories have circulated about many other UFO crashes which the US government has more successfully quashed, a number of which have been in New Mexico. This corner of the USA has been the scene of many nuclear-related operations, including the first atomic test. It is well known that alien craft have been particularly interested in examining various nuclear test facilities, missile sites and airbases which housed nuclear weapons – Bentwaters (*see* chapter 3) was one such base. There have even been unconfirmed stories of missile warheads at one site having been neutralized.

The most active and professional UFO research activity has taken place in the USA. Ufologists in the forefront of the hunt for hard evidence of alien visitors have taken two primary directions. One has been to follow up, co-ordinate and check the more significant sightings. The other has been to attempt to persuade the US government to admit that it has significant material on UFOs, sightings and contacts. Their efforts have met with limited success, even with the assistance of the Freedom of Information Act. Even documents that have been made available to researchers have large sections deleted. In itself this would suggest that the government does indeed have something to hide.

THE ROSWELL COVER-UP

The first real chink in the armour of government secrecy came when UFO investigator Jaime Shandera received a roll of undeveloped 35mm film anonymously hand delivered to his front door in December 1984. It consisted of eight pages of a secret document, dated 18 November 1952, which briefed President-Elect Eisenhower about UFOs and Roswell. It also detailed the creation and existence of a high-level group of scientists and military men, referred to as Majestic-12, which reported directly to the President, and whose task was to co-ordinate policy and activity towards alien visitors and their craft.

The document provides the names of the 12 men who comprised MJ-1 to 12 within the Majestic-12 operation. The text of seven of the eight pages is reproduced in full below. Page 7, titled simply 'Appendix A', has been omitted.

BRIEFING DOCUMENT: OPERATION MAJESTIC-12

PREPARED FOR PRESIDENT-ELECT DWIGHT D
EISENHOWER (EYES ONLY)
18 NOVEMBER, 1952

WARNING: This is a TOP SECRET – EYES ONLY document containing compartmentalized information essential to the national security of the United States. EYES ONLY ACCESS to the material herein is strictly limited to those possessing Majestic-12 clearance level. Reproduction in any form or the taking of written or mechanically transcribed notes is strictly forbidden.

★★★★★★★★★★★★★★★★
★TOP SECRET★
★★★★★★★★★★★★★★★★

SUBJECT: OPERATION MAJESTIC-12 PRELIMINARY
BRIEFING FOR
PRESIDENT-ELECT EISENHOWER.

DOCUMENT PREPARED 18 NOVEMBER, 1952.

BRIEFING OFFICER:
ADM ROSCOE H HILLENKOETTER (MJ-1)

NOTE: This document has been prepared as a preliminary
briefing only. It should be regarded as introductory to a full
operations briefing intended to follow.

******

OPERATION MAJESTIC-12 is a TOP SECRET Research
and Development/Intelligence operation responsible directly
and only to the President of the United States. Operations of
the project are carried out under control of the Majestic-12
(Majic-12) Group which was established by special classified
executive order of President Truman on 24 September, 1947,
upon recommendation by Dr Vannevar Bush and Secretary
James Forrestal. (See Attachment 'A'.) Members of the
Majestic-12 Group were designated as follows:

> Adm Roscoe H Hillenkoetter
> Dr Vannevar Bush
> Secy James V Forrestal
> Gen Nathan F Twining
> Gen Hoyt S Vandenberg
> Dr Detlev Bronk
> Dr Jerome Hunsaker
> Mr Sidney W Souers
> Mr Gordon Gray
> Dr Donald Menzel
> Gen Robert M Montague
> Dr Lloyd V Berkner

The death of Secretary Forrestal on 22 May, 1949, created a
vacancy which remained unfilled until 01 August, 1950, upon

which date Gen Walter B Smith was designated as permanent replacement.

****
TOP SECRET
****

On 24 June, 1947, a civilian pilot, flying over the Cascade Mountains in the State of Washington observed nine flying disc-shaped aircraft traveling in formation at a high rate of speed. Although this was not the first known sighting of such objects, it was the first to gain widespread attention in the public media. Hundreds of reports of sightings of similar objects followed. Many of these came from highly credible military and civilian sources. These reports resulted in independent efforts by several different elements of the military to ascertain the nature and purpose of these objects in the interests of national defense. A number of witnesses were interviewed and there were several unsuccessful attempts to utilize aircraft in efforts to pursue reported discs in flight. Public reaction bordered on near hysteria at times.

In spite of these efforts, little of substance was learned about the objects until a local rancher reported that one had crashed in a remote region of New Mexico located approximately seventy-five miles northwest of Roswell Army Air Base (now Walker Field).

On 07 July, 1947, a secret operation was begun to assure recovery of the wreckage of this object for scientific study. During the course of this operation, aerial reconnaissance discovered that four small human-like beings had apparently ejected from the craft at some point before it exploded. These had fallen to earth about two miles east of the wreckage site. All four were dead and badly decomposed due to action by predators and exposure to the elements during the approximately one week time period which had elapsed before their discovery. A special scientific team took charge of removing these bodies for study. (See Attachment 'C'.) The wreckage of the craft was also removed to several different locations. (See Attachment 'B'.) Civilian and military witnesses in the area were debriefed, and news reporters were given the effective cover story that the object had been a misguided weather research balloon.

****
TOP SECRET
****

A covert analytical effort organized by Gen Twining and Dr Bush acting on the direct orders of the President, resulted in a preliminary consensus (19 September, 1947) that the disc was most likely a short range reconnaissance craft. This conclusion was based for the most part on the craft's size and the apparent lack of any identifiable provisioning. (See Attachment 'D'.) A similar analysis of the four dead occupants was arranged by Dr Bronk. It was the tentative conclusion of this group (30 November, 1947) that although these creatures are human-like in appearance, the biological and evolutionary processes responsible for their development has apparently been quite different from those observed or postulated in homo-sapiens. Dr Bronk's team has suggested the term 'Extraterrestrial Biological Entities', or 'EBEs', be adopted as the standard term of reference for these creatures until such time as a more definitive designation can be agreed upon.

Since it is virtually certain that these craft do not originate in any country on earth, considerable speculation has centered around what their point of origin may be and how they get here. Mars was and remains a possibility, although some scientists, most notably Dr Menzel, consider it more likely that we are dealing with beings from another solar system entirely.

Numerous examples of what appear to be a form of writing were found in the wreckage. Efforts to decipher these have remained largely unsuccessful. (See Attachment 'E'.) Equally unsuccessful have been efforts to determine the methods of propulsion or the nature or method of transmission of the power source involved. Research along these lines has been complicated by the complete absence of identifiable wings, propellers, jets, or other conventional methods of propulsion and guidance, as well as a total lack of metallic wiring, vacuum tubes, or similar recognizable electronic components. (See Attachment 'F'.) It is assumed that the propulsion unit was completely destroyed by the explosion which caused the crash.

****
TOP SECRET
****

A need for as much additional information as possible about these craft, their performance characteristics and their purpose led to the undertaking known as US Air Force Project SIGN in December, 1947. In order to preserve security, liaison between SIGN and Majestic-12 was limited to two individuals within the Intelligence Division of Air Material Command whose role was to pass along certain types of information through channels. SIGN evolved into Project GRUDGE in December, 1948. The operation is currently being conducted under the code name BLUE BOOK, with liaison maintained through the Air Force officer who is head of the project.

On 06 December, 1950, a second object, probably of similar origin, impacted the earth at high speed in the El Indio–Guerrero area of Texas–Mexican border after following a long trajectory through the atmosphere. By the time a search team arrived, what remained of the object had been totally incinerated. Such material as could be recovered was transported to the A.E.C. facility at Sandia, New Mexico, for study.

Implications for the National Security are of continuing importance in that the motives and ultimate intentions of these visitors remain completely unknown. In addition, a significant upsurge in the surveillance activity of these craft beginning in May and continuing through the autumn of this year has caused considerable concern that new developments may be imminent. It is for these reasons, as well as the obvious international and technological considerations and the ultimate need to avoid a public panic at all costs, that the Majestic-12 Group remains of the unanimous opinion that imposition of the strictest security precautions should continue without interruption into the new administration. At the same time, contingency plan MJ-1949-04P/78 (Top Secret – Eyes Only) should be held in continued readiness should the need to make a public announcement present itself. (See Attachment 'G'.)

```
****************
* TOP SECRET *
****************
```

ENUMERATION OF ATTACHMENTS

*ATTACHMENT 'A' . . . Special Classified Executive
Order #092447.
(TS/EO)

*ATTACHMENT 'B' . . . Operation Majestic-12 Status
Report #1, Part A. 30 NOV '47.
(TS-MAJIC/EO)

*ATTACHMENT 'C' . . . Operation Majestic-12 Status
Report #1, Part B. 30 NOV '47.
(TS-MAJIC/EO)

*ATTACHMENT 'D' . . Operation Majestic-12 Preliminary
Analytical Report. 19 SEP '47.
(TS-MAJIC/EO)

*ATTACHMENT 'E' . . . Operation Majestic-12 Blue Team
Report #5. 30 JUN '52.
(TS-MAJIC/EO)

*ATTACHMENT 'F' . . . Operation Majestic-12 Status
Report #2. 31 JAN '48.
(TS-MAJIC/EO)

*ATTACHMENT 'G' . . . Operation Majestic-12
Contingency Plan MJ-1949-04P/78: 31 JAN '49.
(TS-MAJIC/EO)

*ATTACHMENT 'H' . . . Operation Majestic-12, Maps and
Photographs Folio (Extractions).
(TS-MAJIC/EO)

```
****************
* TOP SECRET *
****************
```

MEMORANDUM FOR THE SECRETARY OF DEFENSE

Dear Secretary Forrestal:

As per our recent conversation on this matter, you are hereby authorized to proceed with all due speed and caution upon your undertaking. Hereafter this matter shall be referred to only as Operation Majestic Twelve.

It continues to be my feeling that any future considerations relative to the ultimate disposition of this matter should rest solely with the Office of the President following appropriate discussions with yourself, Dr Bush and the Director of Central Intelligence.

[signature of Harry Truman]

```
****************
* TOP SECRET *
****************
```

EYES ONLY

THE US AIR FORCE TEXTBOOK *INTRODUCTORY SPACE SCIENCE*

Since the appearance of this document UFO investigators following the route of government disclosure have had minimal success, regardless of the Freedom of Information Act and several requests from their state senators. The researchers who followed the government 'paper trail' of memos and briefing documents have had marginally more success. Their stories have been told numerous times in books which read like detective stories. The stories are reminiscent of Watergate and 'Deep Throat' – the secret informer within the government. Some ufologists have referred to this hunt as a 'Cosmic Watergate'.

Inside information in the quest has often come about as a

result of insiders making whole documents available. One of the most significant was a United States Air Force textbook entitled *Introductory Space Science*, edited by Major Donald G Carpenter and co-edited by Lieutenant Colonel Edward R Therkelson. It was used by the Air Force Academy at Colorado Springs, Colorado, but withdrawn from circulation in the early 1970s. It was acquired by Michael Corbin's ParaNet Information Services in 1989.

Chapter XXIII, which deals with 'Unidentified Flying Objects' was transcribed by Don Ecker, ParaNet's Research Director. It is so interesting to find such an informative military textbook and training manual, written with such candour about UFOs, that I quote the relevant chapter in full so that readers can see for themselves the attitude of the Air Force towards this phenomenon.

What is an Unidentified Flying Object (UFO)? Well, according to United States Air Force Regulation 80–17 (dated 19 September 1966), a UFO is 'Any aerial phenomenon or object which is unknown or appears to be out of the ordinary to the observer.' This is a very broad definition which applies equally well to one individual seeing his first noctilucent cloud at twilight as it does to another individual seeing his first helicopter. However, at present most people consider the term UFO to mean an object which behaves in a strange or erratic manner while moving through the Earth's atmosphere. That strange phenomenon has evoked strong emotions and great curiosity among a large segment of our world's population. The average person is interested because he loves a mystery, the professional military man is involved because of the possible threat to national security, and some scientists are interested because of the basic curiosity that led them into becoming researchers.

The literature on UFOs is so vast, and the stories so many and varied, that we can only present a sketchy outline of the subject in this chapter. That outline includes description classifications, operational domains (temporal and spatial), some theories as to the nature of the UFO phenomenon, human reactions, attempts to attack the problem scientifically, and some tentative conclusions. If you wish to read further in this area, the references provide an excellent starting point.

33.1 Descriptions
One of the greatest problems you encounter when attempting to catalog UFO sightings, is selection of a system for cataloging. No effective system has yet been devised, although a number of different systems have been proposed. The net result is that almost all UFO data are either treated in the form of individual cases, or in the form of inadequate classification systems. However, these systems do tend to have some common factors, and a collection of these factors is as follows:

a Size
b Shape (disc, ellipse, football, etc)
c Luminosity
d Color
e Number of UFOs

Behavior
a Location (altitude, direction, etc)
b Patterns of paths (straight line, climbing, zig-zagging, etc)
c Flight characteristics (wobbling, fluttering, etc)
d Periodicity of sightings
e Time duration
f Curiosity or inquisitiveness
g Avoidance
h Hostility

Associated effects
a Electro-Magnetic (compass, radio, ignition systems, etc)
b Radiation (burns, induced radioactivity, etc)
c Ground disturbance (dust stirred up, leaves moved, standing wave peaks of surface of water, etc)
d Sound (none, hissing, humming, roaring, thunderclaps, etc)
e Vibration (weak, strong, slow, fast)
f Smell (ozone or other odor)
g Flame (how much, where, when, color)
h Smoke or cloud (amount, color, persistence)
i Debris (type, amount, color, persistence)
j Inhibition of voluntary movement by observers
k Sighting of 'creatures' or 'beings'

After effects
   a Burned areas or animals
   b Depressed or flattened areas
   c Dead or 'missing' animals
   d Mentally disturbed people
   e Missing items

We make no attempt here to present available data in terms of the foregoing descriptors.

33.2 Operational domains – temporal and spatial

What we will do here is to present evidence that UFOs are a global phenomenon which may have persisted for many thousands of years. During this discussion, please remember that the more ancient the reports the less sophisticated the observer. Not only were the ancient observers lacking the terminology necessary to describe complex devices (such as present day helicopters) but they were also lacking the concepts necessary to understand the true nature of such things as television, spaceships, rockets, nuclear weapons and radiation effects. To some, the most advanced technological concept was a war chariot with knife blades attached to the wheels. By the same token, the very lack of accurate terminology and descriptions leaves the more ancient reports open to considerable misinterpretation, and it may well be that present evaluations of individual reports are completely wrong. Nevertheless, let us start with an intriguing story in one of the oldest chronicles of India . . . the Book of Dzyan.

The book is a group of 'story-teller' legends which were finally gathered in manuscript form when man learned to write. One of the stories is of a small group of beings who supposedly came to Earth many thousands of years ago in a metal craft which orbited the Earth several times before landing. As told in the Book 'These beings lived to themselves and were revered by the humans among whom they had settled. But eventually differences arose among them and they divided their numbers, several of the men and women and some children settled in another city, where they were promptly installed as rulers by the awe-stricken populace.

'Separation did not bring peace to these people and finally their anger reached a point where the ruler of the original city took with him a small number of his warriors and they rose into the air in a huge shining metal vessel. While they were many leagues from the city of their enemies, they launched a great shining lance that rode on a beam of light. It burst apart in the city of their enemies with a great ball of flame that shot up to the heavens, almost to the stars. All those who were in the city were horribly burned and even those who were not in the city – but nearby – were burned also. Those who looked upon the lance and the ball of fire were blinded forever afterward. Those who entered the city on foot became ill and died. Even the dust of the city was poisoned, as were the rivers that flowed through it. Men dared not go near it, and it gradually crumbled into dust and was forgotten by men.

'When the leader saw what he had done to his own people he retired to his palace and refused to see anyone. Then he gathered about him those warriors who remained, and their wives and children, and they entered their vessels and rose one by one into the sky and sailed away. Nor did they return.'

Could this foregoing legend really be an account of an extra-terrestrial colonization, complete with guided missile, nuclear warhead and radiation effects? It is difficult to assess the validity of that explanation . . . just as it is difficult to explain why Greek, Roman and Nordic Mythology all discuss wars and contacts among their 'Gods.' (Even the Bible records conflict between the legions of God and Satan.) Could it be that each group recorded their parochial view of what was actually a global conflict among alien colonists or visitors? Or is it that man has led such a violent existence that he tends to expect conflict and violence among even his gods?

Evidence of perhaps an even earlier possible contact was uncovered by Tschi Pen Lao of the University of Peking. He discovered astonishing carvings in granite on a mountain in Hunan Province and on an island in Lake Tungting. These carvings have been evaluated as 47,000 years old, and they show people with large trunks (breathing apparatus? . . . or 'elephant' heads shown on human bodies? Remember, the Egyptians often represented their gods as animal heads on human bodies.)

Only 8,000 years ago, rocks were sculpted in the Tassili plateau of Sahara, depicting what appeared to be human beings but with strange round heads (helmets? or 'sun' heads on human bodies?) And even more recently, in the Bible, Genesis (6:4) tells of angels from the sky mating with women of Earth, who bore them children. Genesis 19:3 tells of Lot meeting two angels in the desert and his later feeding them at his house. The Bible also tells a rather unusual story of Ezekiel who witnessed what has been interpreted by some to have been a spacecraft or aircraft landing near the Chebar River in Chaldea (593 BC).

Even the Irish have recorded strange visitations. In the Speculum Regali in Konungs Skuggsa (and other accounts of the era about 956 AD) are numerous stories of 'demonships' in the skies. In one case a rope from one such ship became entangled with part of a church. A man from the ship climbed down the rope to free it, but was seized by the townspeople. The Bishop made the people release the man, who climbed back to the ship, where the crew cut the rope and the ship rose and sailed out of sight. In all of his actions, the climbing man appeared as if he were swimming in water. Stories such as this make one wonder if the legends of the 'little people' of Ireland were based upon imagination alone.

About the same time, in Lyons (France) three men and a woman supposedly descended from an airship or spaceship and were captured by a mob. These foreigners admitted to being wizards, and were killed. (No mention is made of the methods employed to extract the admissions.) Many documented UFO sightings occurred throughout the Middle Ages, including an especially startling one of a UFO over London on 16 December 1742. However, we do not have room to include any more of the Middle Ages sightings. Instead, two 'more-recent' sightings are contained in this section to bring us up to modern times.

In a sworn statement dated 21 April 1897, a prosperous and prominent farmer named Alexander Hamilton (Le Roy, Kansas, USA) told of an attack upon his cattle at about 10.30 pm the previous Monday. He, his son, and his tenant grabbed axes and ran some 700 feet from the house to the cow lot where a great cigar-shaped ship about 300 feet long floated some 30 feet above his cattle. It had a carriage underneath which was brightly lighted within (dirigible and gondola?) and which had numerous windows. Inside were six strange looking beings jabbering in a foreign language. These beings suddenly became aware of Hamilton and the others. They immediately turned a searchlight on the farmer, and also turned on some power which sped up a turbine wheel (about 30 feet diameter) located under the craft. The ship rose, taking with it a two-year-old heifer which was roped about the neck by a cable of one-half inch thick, red material. The next day a neighbor, Link Thomas, found the animal's hide, legs and head in his field. He was mystified at how the remains got to where they were because of the lack of tracks in the soft soil. Alexander Hamilton's sworn statement was accompanied by an affidavit as to his veracity. The affidavit was signed by ten of the local leading citizens.

On the evening of 4 November 1957 at Fort Itaipu, Brazil, two sentries noted a 'new star' in the sky. The 'star' grew in size and within seconds stopped over the fort. It drifted slowly downward, was as large as a big aircraft, and was surrounded by a strong orange glow. A distinct humming sound was heard, and then the heat struck. A sentry collapsed almost immediately, the other managed to slide to shelter under the heavy cannons where his loud cries awoke the garrison. While the troops were scrambling towards their battle stations, complete electrical failure occurred. There was panic until the lights came back on but a number of men still managed to see an orange glow leaving the area at high speed. Both sentries were found badly burned . . . one unconscious and the other incoherent, suffering from deep shock.

Thus, UFO sightings not only appear to extend back 47,000 years through time but also are global in nature. One has the feeling that this phenomenon deserves some sort of valid scientific investigation, even if it is a low level effort.

33.3 Some theories as to the nature of the UFO phenomenon

There are very few cohesive theories as to the nature of UFOs. Those theories that have been advanced can be collected in five groups:

a Mysticism
b Hoaxes and rantings due to unstable personalities
c Secret weapons
d Natural phenomena
e Alien visitors

Mysticism

It is believed by some cults that the mission of UFOs and their crews is a spiritual one, and that all materialistic efforts to determine the UFOs' nature are doomed to failure.

Hoaxes and rantings due to unstable personalities

Some have suggested that all UFO reports were the results of pranks and hoaxes, or were made by people with unstable personalities. This attitude was particularly prevalent during the time period when the Air Force investigation was being operated under the code name of Project Grudge. A few airlines even went as far as to ground every pilot who reported seeing a 'flying saucer.' The only way for the pilot to regain flight status was to undergo a psychiatric examination. There was a noticeable decline in pilot reports during this time interval, and a few interpreted this decline to prove that UFOs were either hoaxes or the result of unstable personalities. It is of interest that NICAP (The National Investigations Committee on Aerial Phenomena) even today still receives reports from commercial pilots who neglect to notify either the Air Force or their own airline.

There are a number of cases which indicate that not all reports fall in the hoax category. We will examine one such case now. It is the Socorro, New Mexico, sighting made by police Sergeant Lonnie Zamora. Sergeant Zamora was patrolling the streets of Socorro on 24 April 1964 when he saw a shiny object drift down into an area of gullies on the edge of town. He also heard a loud roaring noise which sounded as if an old dynamite shed located out that way had exploded. He immediately radioed police headquarters, and drove out toward the shed. Zamora was forced to stop about 150 yards away from a deep gully in which there appeared to be an overturned car. He radioed that he was investigating a possible wreck, and then worked his car up onto the mesa and over toward the edge of the gully. He parked short, and when he walked the final few feet to the edge, he was amazed to see that it was not a car but instead was a weird eggshaped object about 15 feet long, white in color and resting on short, metal legs. Beside it, unaware of his presence, were two humanoids dressed in silvery coveralls. They seemed to be working on a portion of the underside of the object. Zamora was still standing there, surprised, when they suddenly noticed him and dove out of sight around the object. Zamora also headed the other way, back toward his car. He glanced back at the object just as a bright blue flame shot down from the underside. Within seconds the eggshaped thing rose out of the gully with 'an earsplitting roar.' The object was out of sight over the nearby mountains almost immediately, and

Sergeant Zamora was moving the opposite direction almost as fast when he met Sergeant Sam Chavez who was responding to Zamora's earlier radio calls. Together they investigated the gully and found the bushes charred and still smoking where the blue flame had jetted down on them. About the charred area were four deep marks where the metal legs had been. Each mark was three and one half inches deep, and was circular in shape. The sand in the gully was very hard packed so no sign of the humanoids' footprints could be found. An official investigation was launched that same day, and all data obtained supported the stories of Zamora and Chavez. It is rather difficult to label this episode a hoax, and it is also doubtful that both Zamora and Chavez shared portions of the same hallucination.

Secret weapons
A few individuals have proposed that UFOs are actually advanced weapon systems, and that their natures must not be revealed. Very few people accept this as a credible suggestion.

Natural phenomena
It has also been suggested that at least some, and possibly all of the UFO cases were just misinterpreted manifestations of natural phenomena. Undoubtedly this suggestion has some merit. People have reported, as UFOs, objects which were conclusively proven to be balloons (weather and skyhook), the planet Venus, man-made artificial satellites, normal aircraft, unusual cloud formations, and lights from ceilometers (equipment projecting light beams on cloud bases to determine the height of the aircraft visual ceiling). It is also suspected that people have reported mirages, optical illusions, swamp gas and ball lightning (a poorly-understood discharge of electrical energy in a spheroidal or ellipsoidal shape . . . some charges have lasted for up to fifteen minutes but the ball is usually no bigger than a large orange.) But it is difficult to tell a swamp dweller that the strange, fast-moving light he saw in the sky was swamp gas; and it is just as difficult to tell a farmer that a bright UFO in the sky is the same ball lightning that he has seen rolling along his fence wires in dry weather. Thus accidental misidentification of what might well be natural phenomena breeds mistrust and disbelief; it leads to the hasty conclusion that the truth is deliberately not being told. One last suggestion of interest has been made, that the UFOs were plasmoids from space . . .

concentrated blobs of solar wind that succeeded in reaching the surface of the Earth. Somehow this last suggestion does not seem to be very plausible; perhaps because it ignores such things as penetration of Earth's magnetic field.

Alien visitors

The most stimulating theory for us is that the UFOs are material objects which are either 'manned' or remote-controlled by beings who are alien to this planet. There is some evidence supporting this viewpoint. In addition to police Sergeant Lonnie Zamora's experience, let us consider the case of Barney and Betty Hill. On a trip through New England they lost two hours on the night of 19 September 1961 without even realizing it. However, after that night both Barney and Betty began developing psychological problems which eventually grew sufficiently severe that they submitted themselves to psychiatric examination and treatment. During the course of treatment hypnotherapy was used, and it yielded remarkably detailed and similar stories from both Barney and Betty. Essentially they had been hypnotically kidnapped, taken aboard a UFO, submitted to two-hour physicals, and released with posthypnotic suggestions to forget the entire incident. The evidence is rather strong that this is what the Hills, even in their subconscious, believe happened to them. And it is of particular importance that after the 'posthypnotic block' was removed, both of the Hills ceased having their psychological problems.

The Hills' description of the aliens was similar to descriptions provided in other cases, but this particular type of alien appears to be in the minority. The most commonly described alien is about three and one half feet tall, has a round head (helmet?), arms reaching to or below his knees, and is wearing a silvery space suit or coveralls. Other aliens appear to be essentially the same as Earthmen, while still others have particularity wide (wrap around) eyes and mouths with very thin lips. And there is a rare group reported as about four feet tall, weight of around 35 pounds, and covered with thick hair or fur (clothing?). Members of this last group are described as being extremely strong. If such beings are visiting Earth, two questions arise: 1) why haven't they attempted to contact us officially? . . . The answer to the first question may exist partially in Sergeant Lonnie Zamora's experience, and may exist partially in the Tunguska meteor discussed in Chapter XXIX. In that chapter it was suggested that the Tunguska meteor was actually a comet which exploded in the atmosphere, the ices melted and the dust spread out. Hence, no debris. However, it has also been suggested that the Tunguska meteor was actually an alien space-craft that entered the atmosphere too rapidly, suffered mechanical failure, and lost its power supply and/or weapons in a nuclear explosion. While that hypothesis may seem far fetched, samples of tree rings from around the world reveal that, immediately after the Tunguska meteor explosion, the level of radioactivity in the world rose sharply for a short period of time. It is difficult to find a natural explanation for that increase in radioactivity, although the suggestion has been advanced that enough of the meteor's great kinetic energy was converted into heat (by atmospheric friction) that a fusion reaction occurred. This still leaves us with no answer to the second question: why no contact? That question is very easy to answer in several ways: 1) we may be the object of intensive sociological and psychological study. In such studies you usually avoid disturbing the test subjects' environment; 2) you do not 'contact' a colony of ants, and humans may seem that way to any aliens (variation: a zoo is fun to visit, but you don't 'contact' the lizards); 3) such contact may have already taken place secretly; and 4) such contact may have already taken place on a different plane of awareness and we are not yet sensitive to communications on such a plane. These are just a few of the reasons. You may add to the list as you desire.

33.4 Human fear and hostility

Besides the foregoing reasons, contacting humans is downright dangerous. Think about that for a moment! On the microscopic level our bodies reject and fight (through production of antibodies) any alien material; this process helps us fight off disease but it also sometimes results in allergic reactions to innocuous materials. On the macroscopic (psychological and sociological) level we are antagonistic to beings that are 'different.' For proof of that, just watch how an odd child is treated by other children, or how a minority group is socially deprived, or how the Arabs feel about the Israelis (Chinese vs Japanese, Turks vs Greeks, etc.) In case you are hesitant to extend that concept to the treatment of aliens let me point out that in very ancient times, possible extraterrestrials may have been treated as gods but in the last two thousand years, the evidence is that any possible aliens have been ripped apart by mobs, shot and shot at, physically assaulted, and in general treated with fear and aggression.

In Ireland about 1000 AD, supposed airships were treated as 'demonships.' In Lyons, France, 'admitted' space travellers were killed. More recently, on 24 July 1957 Russian anti-aircraft batteries on the Kouril Islands opened fire on UFOs. Although all Soviet anti-aircraft batteries on the Islands were in action, no hits were made. The UFOs were luminous and moved very fast. We too have fired on UFOs. About ten o'clock one morning, a radar site near a fighter base picked up a UFO doing 700 mph. The UFO then slowed to 100 mph, and two F-86s were scrambled to intercept. Eventually one F-86 closed on the UFO at about 3,000 feet altitude. The UFO began to accelerate away but the pilot still managed to get within 500 yards of the target for a short period of time. It was definitely saucer shaped. As the pilot pushed the F-86 at top speed, the UFO began to pull away. When the range reached 1,000 yards, the pilot armed his guns and fired in an attempt to down the saucer. He failed, and the UFO pulled away rapidly, vanishing in the distance. This same basic situation may have happened on a more personal level. On Sunday evening 21 August 1955, eight adults and three children were on the Sutton Farm (one-half mile from Kelly, Kentucky) when, according to them, one of the children saw a brightly glowing UFO settle behind the barn, out of sight from where he stood. Other witnesses on nearby farms also saw the object. However, the Suttons dismissed it as a 'shooting star', and did not investigate. Approximately thirty minutes later (at 8.00 pm), the family dogs began barking so two of the men went to the back door and looked out. Approximately 50 feet away and coming toward them was a creature wearing a glowing silvery suit. It was about three and one-half feet tall with a large round head and very long arms. It had large webbed hands which were equipped with claws. The two Suttons grabbed a twelve gauge shotgun and a ·22 caliber pistol, and fired at close range. They could hear the pellets and bullets ricochet as if off of metal. The creature was knocked down, but jumped up and scrambled away. The Suttons retreated into the house, turned off all inside lights, and turned on the porch light. At that moment, one of the women who was peeking out of the dining room window discovered that a creature with some sort of helmet and wide slit eyes was peeking back at her. She screamed, the men rushed in and started shooting. The creature was knocked backwards but again scrambled away without apparent harm. More shooting occurred (a total of about 50 rounds) over the next 20 minutes and the creatures finally left (perhaps feeling unwelcome?) After about a two hour wait (for safety), the Suttons left too. By the time the police got there, the aliens were gone but the Suttons would not move back to the farm. They sold it and departed. This reported incident does bear out the contention though that humans are dangerous. At no time in the story did the supposed aliens shoot back, although one is left with the impression that the described creatures were having fun scaring humans.

33.5 Attempts at scientific approaches

In any scientific endeavor, the first step is to acquire data, the second step to classify the data, and the third step to form hypotheses. The hypotheses are tested by repeating the entire process, with each cycle resulting in an increase in understanding (we hope). The UFO phenomenon does not yield readily to this approach because the data taken so far exhibits both excessive variety and vagueness. The vagueness is caused in part by the lack of preparation of the observer . . . very few people leave their house knowing that they are going to see a UFO that evening. Photographs are overexposed or underexposed, and rarely in color. Hardly anyone carries around a radiation counter or magnetometer. And, in addition to this, there is a very high level of 'noise' in the data.

The noise consists of mistaken reports of known natural phenomena, hoaxes, reports by unstable individuals and mistaken removal of data regarding possible unnatural or unknown natural phenomena (by overzealous individuals who are trying to eliminate all data due to known natural phenomena). In addition, those data which do appear to be valid, exhibit an excessive amount of variety relative to the statistical samples which are available. This has led to very clumsy classification systems, which in turn provide quite unfertile ground for formulation of hypotheses.

One hypothesis which looked promising for a time was that of ORTHOTENY (ie UFO sightings fall on 'great circle' routes). At first, plots of sightings seemed to verify the concept of orthoteny but recent use of computers has revealed that even random numbers yield 'great circle' plots as neatly as do UFO sightings.

There is one solid advance that has been made though. Jacques and Janine Vallee have taken a particular type of UFO – namely those that are lower than tree-top level when sighted – and plotted the UFO's estimated diameter versus the estimated distance from the observer. The result yields an average diameter of 5 meters with a very characteristic drop for short viewing distances. This behavior at the extremes of the curve is well known to astronomers and psychologists as the 'moon illusion.' The illusion only occurs when the object being viewed is a real, physical object. Because this implies that the observers have viewed a real object, it permits us to accept also their statement that these particular UFOs had a rotational axis of symmetry.

Another, less solid, advance made by the Vallees was their plotting of the total number of sightings per week versus the date. They did this for the time span from 1947 to 1962, and then attempted to match the peaks of the curve (every 2 years 2 months) to the times of Earth–Mars conjunction (every 2 years 1.4 months). The match was very good between 1950 and 1956 but was poor outside those limits. Also, the peaks were not only at the times of Earth–Mars conjunction but also roughly at the first harmonic (very loosely, every 13 months). This raises the question why should UFOs only visit Earth when Mars is in conjunction and when it is on the opposite side of the sun. Obviously, the conjunction periodicity of Mars is not the final answer. As it happens, there is an interesting possibility to consider. Suppose Jupiter's conjunctions were used; they are every 13.1 months. That would satisfy the observed periods nicely, except for every even data peak being of different magnitude from every odd data peak. Perhaps a combination of Martian, Jovian, and Saturnian (and even other planetary) conjunctions will be necessary to match the frequency plot . . . if it can be matched.

Further data correlation is quite difficult. There are a large number of different saucer shapes but this may mean little. For example, look at the number of different types of aircraft which are in use in the US Air Force alone.

It is obvious that intensive scientific study is needed in this area; no such study has yet been undertaken at the necessary levels of intensity needed. Something that must be guarded against in any such study is the trap of implicitly assuming that our knowledge of physics (or any other branch of science) is complete. An example of one such trap is selecting a group of physical laws which we now accept as valid, and assuming that they will never be superseded.

Five such laws might be:

1 Every action must have an opposite and equal reaction.
2 Every particle in the universe attracts every other particle with a force proportional to the product of the masses and inversely as the square of the distance.
3 Energy, mass and momentum are conserved.
4 No material body can have a speed as great as c, the speed of light in free space.
5 The maximum energy, E, which can be obtained from a body at rest is $E=mc^2$, where m is the rest mass of the body.

Laws numbered 1 and 3 seem fairly safe, but let us hesitate and take another look. Actually, law number 3 is only valid (now) from a relativistic viewpoint; and for that matter so are laws 4 and 5. But relativity completely revised these physical concepts after 1915, before then Newtonian mechanics were supreme. We should also note that general relativity has not yet been verified. Thus we have the peculiar situation of five laws which appear to deny the possibility of intelligent alien control of UFOs, yet three of the laws are recent in concept and may not even be valid. Also, law number 2 has not yet been tested under conditions of large relative speeds or accelerations. We should not deny the possibility of alien control of UFOs on the basis of preconceived notions not established as related or relevant to the UFOs.

33.6 Conclusion

From available information, the UFO phenomenon appears to have been global in nature for almost 50,000 years. The majority of known witnesses have been reliable people who have seen easily-explained natural phenomena, and there appears to be no overall positive correlation with population density. The entire phenomenon could be psychological in nature but that is quite doubtful. However, psychological factors probably do enter the data picture as 'noise.' The phenomenon could also be entirely due to known and unknown phenomena (with some psychological 'noise' added in) but that too is questionable in view of some of the available data.

This leaves us with the unpleasant possibility of alien visitors to our planet, or at least of alien controlled UFOs. However, the data are not well correlated, and what questionable data there are suggest the existence of at least three and maybe four different groups of aliens (possibly at different states of development). This too is difficult to accept. It implies the existence of intelligent life on a majority of the planets in our solar system, or a surprisingly strong interest in Earth by members of other solar systems.

A solution to the UFO problem may be obtained by the long and diligent effort of a large group of well financed and competent scientists, unfortunately there is no evidence suggesting that such an effort is going to be made. However, even if such an effort were made, there is no guarantee of success because of the isolated and sporadic nature of the sightings. Also, there may be nothing to find, and that would mean a long search with no profit at the end. The best thing to do is to keep an open and skeptical mind, and not take an extreme position on any side of the question.

THE MJ-12 SPECIAL OPERATIONS MANUAL ON THE RECOVERY AND DISPOSAL OF ALIENS

After the appearance of the *Introductory Space Science* document in the public arena in 1989, there was a lull as further inside information dried up to a trickle – until December 1994, when Don Berliner received a roll of 35mm film in a manila envelope, posted in Wisconsin, without a return address. It consisted of photographs of eighteen pages from a Majestic-12 Group special operations manual. The full text of the manual is available in Stanton Friedman's book *Top Secret/Majic*, in which he evaluates the authenticity of the document.

The objective of the manual, which is dated April 1954, is quite clear from the title: *Extraterrestial Entities and Technology, Recovery and Disposal*. Under Section 1, which deals with 'Project Purpose and Goals', the importance of the subject is stressed.

MJ-12 takes the subject of UFOBs, Extraterrestrial Technology and Extraterrestrial Biological Entities very seriously and considers the entire subject to be a matter of the very highest national security. For that reason everything relating the subject has been assigned the very highest security classification.

The reason for the high level of secrecy and the paucity of information regarding the Majestic-12 Group is perhaps made clear in the next subsection.

All information relating to MJ-12 has been classified MAJIC EYES ONLY and carries a security level 2 points above that of Top Secret. The reason for this has to do with the consequences that may arise not only from the impact upon the public should the existence of such matters become general knowledge, but also the danger of having such advanced technology as has been recovered by the Air Force fall into the hands of unfriendly foreign powers. *No information is released to the public press* [my emphasis] and the official position is that no special group such as MJ-12 exists.

The US government was understandably wary of having to deal with this strange and inexplicable new phenomenon. It had just won a major war in which breaking the supposedly secure codes of its Pacific enemy played a major role. Security was integral to its success. And now as the Cold War was beginning to heat up, here were unidentified craft probing the skies above the very area where the ultimate weapon that finally caused the Japanese to admit defeat was developed – Los Alamos, New Mexico. It was unclear in 1954 what technology the Soviet Union might use to enforce its will on its enemies.

In summarizing the current situation for the reader, the manual makes clear the absolute superiority of the technology of the visitors despite the US military having caused 'one of the crashes [as] the result of direct military action'. The document stresses the determination of the US government that such technology should not fall into the hands of its enemies.

It is considered as far as the current situation is concerned, that there are few indications that these objects [UFOs] and their builders pose a direct threat to the security of the United States, despite the uncertainty as to their ultimate motives in coming here. Certainly *the technology possessed by these beings far surpasses anything known to modern science*, [my emphasis] yet their presence here seems to be benign, and they seem to be avoiding contact with our species, at least for the present. Several dead entities have been recovered along with a substantial amount of wreckage and devices from downed craft, all of which are now under study at various locations. No attempt has been made by the extraterrestrial entities either to contact authorities or to recover their dead counterparts of the downed craft, even though one of the crashes was the result of direct military action. *The greatest threat at this time arises from the acquisition and study of such advanced technology by foreign powers unfriendly to the United States* [my emphasis]. It is for this reason that the recovery and study of this type of material by the United States has been given such a high priority.

Given the very real threat of the Cold War breaking out into actual conflict should the Soviet Union gain a massive military advantage over the USA, the sacrifice of the lives and freedom of individual citizens seemed a small price to pay in this global saga. Press freedom seemed almost like a social nicety compared with national survival, as is emphasized in the section of the document that deals with security.

Great care should be taken to preserve the security of any location where Extraterrestrial Technology might be retrievable for scientific study. *Extreme measures must be taken* [my emphasis] to protect and preserve any material or craft from discovery, examination, or removal by civilian agencies or individuals of the general public. It is therefore recommended that a total press blackout be initiated whenever possible. If this course of action should not prove feasible, the following cover stories are suggested for release to the press. The officer in charge will act quickly to select the cover story that best fits the situation. It should be remembered when selecting a cover story that *official policy regarding UFOBs is that they do not exist* [my emphasis].

The document goes on to describe the methods to be used to obscure any hint of alien spacecraft or alien visitors, including official denials, discrediting witnesses and the making of deceptive statements. It seems incredible that a government document actually advocates these practices as a matter of policy. The derision with which many witnesses have been treated in the media and by the public can perhaps be traced to the following subsection.

If at all possible, witnesses will be held incommunicado until the extent of their knowledge and involvement can be determined. Witnesses will be discouraged from talking about what they have seen, and *intimidation may be necessary* [my emphasis] to ensure their cooperation. If witnesses have already contacted the press, it will be necessary to discredit their stories. This can best be done by the assertion that they have either misinterpreted natural events, are the victims of hysteria or hallucinations, or are the perpetrators of hoaxes.

This paragraph lends credence to the many stories of witnesses being intimidated, and having their lives threatened by over-zealous MJ-12 agents.

PROJECT BLUE BOOK AND THE CONDON REPORT

In March 1952 Project Blue Book was set up by the US Air Force to co-ordinate reports of UFOs. Its goals were: to find an explanation for all reported sightings of UFOs; to determine if the UFOs posed any threat to the security of the USA; and to determine whether UFOs exhibited technology which could be utilized by the USA.

Many people have subsequently described Project Blue Book as an exercise in public relations, since many of the more 'interesting' sightings and contacts were channelled elsewhere, to an unknown and more secret organization.

After 14 years the Air Force began to tire of Project Blue Book and in 1966 commissioned a report on UFOs from the University of Colorado. This project was headed by Dr Edward Condon, who, it has been recently revealed, held a secret brief to discredit the existence of UFOs. Although the report was titled 'The Scientific Study of Unidentified Flying Objects', it is more commonly referred to as the Condon Report.

It concluded that: there is no evidence that UFOs are extra-terrestrial vehicles; no UFO has ever posed a threat to national security; and there is no evidence that UFOs represent techno-logical developments beyond current scientific knowledge. As a consequence of this 'whitewash' of the subject, the US Air Force closed Project Blue Book in December 1969.

ACKNOWLEDGEMENT OF THE UFO PHENOMENON FROM AROUND THE WORLD

Alien spacecraft are regularly overflying our skies, and the governments of the world are aware of the phenomenon, but as the above examples from the USA show, it has been their deliberate policy to deny it. Below are a number of quotes directly from government sources around the world – people 'in the know' – which show the extent of their acceptance of the reality of UFOs. The significance of their comments is that they are people who have held key military and government positions. Their comments are like beams of light shining through the veil of silence, and only serve to confirm that the policy of silence is one in which all governments are colluding with each other. As General Cavero of the Spanish Air Force said in 1976: 'The nations of the world are currently working together in the investigation of the UFO phenomenon.'

United Kingdom, 1954

More than 10,000 sightings have been reported, the majority of which cannot be accounted for by any 'scientific' explanation . . . I am convinced that these objects do exist and that they are not manufactured by any nation on Earth. I can therefore see no alternative to accepting the theory that they come from some extraterrestrial source. (Air Chief Marshal Lord Dowding, Commander-in-Chief of the Royal Air Force Fighter Command during the Battle of Britain, reprinted in the *Sunday Dispatch*, London, 11 July 1954)

USA, 1957

No agency in this country or Russia is able to duplicate at this time the speeds and accelerations which radars and observers indicate these flying objects are able to achieve . . . There are objects coming into our atmosphere at very high speeds. (Admiral Delmer S Fahrney, former head of the US Navy's guided-missile programme, reported in the *New York Times*, 17 January 1957)

France, 1958

The number of thoughtful, intelligent, educated people in full possession of their faculties who have 'seen something' and described it, grows every day . . . We can . . . say categorically that mysterious objects have indeed appeared and continue to appear in the sky that surrounds us. (General Lionel M Chassin, Commanding General of the French Air Forces, and General Air Defence Co-ordinator of the Allied Air Forces of NATO, in a foreword to Aime Michel's *Flying Saucers and the Straight-Line Mystery*, Criterion Books, 1958)

USA, 1960

It is time for the truth to be brought out . . . Behind the scenes high-ranking Air Force officers are soberly concerned about the UFOs. But through official secrecy and ridicule, many citizens are led to believe the unknown flying objects are nonsense . . . I urge immediate Congressional action to reduce the dangers from secrecy about unidentified flying objects. (Former CIA Director Vice Admiral Roscoe Hillenkoetter, in a signed statement to Congress, 22 August 1960)

Indonesia, 1967

UFOs sighted in Indonesia are identical with those sighted in other countries. Sometimes they pose a problem for our air defense and once we were obliged to open fire on them. (Air Marshall Roesmin Nurjadin, Commander-in-Chief of the Indonesian Air Force, in a letter to Yusuke J Matsumura dated 5 May 1967, reprinted in Timothy Good, *Beyond Top Secret*)

Spain, 1976

I believe that UFOs are spaceships or extraterrestrial craft . . . The nations of the world are currently working together in the investigation of the UFO phenomenon. There is an international exchange of data. Maybe when this group of nations acquires more precise and definite information, it will be possible to release the news to the world. (General Carlos Castro Cavero, General in the Spanish Air Force and former Commander of Spain's Third Aerial Region, in an interview with J J Benitez, *La Gaceta del Norte*, 27 June 1976)

France, 1978

Taking into account the facts that we have gathered from the observers and from the location of their observations, we concluded that there generally can be said to be a material phenomenon behind the observations. In 60% of the cases reported here, the description of this phenomenon is apparently one of a flying machine whose origin, modes of lifting and/or propulsion are totally outside our knowledge. (Dr Claude Poher, founder and first director of GEPAN, the UFO investigative office of the French government's National Centre for Space Sciences, which analysed reports from the Gendarmerie from 1974 to 1978, writing in the GEPAN Report to the Scientific Committee, June 1978, Vol 1, Chapter 4)

USA, 1979

We have, indeed, been contacted – perhaps even visited – by extraterrestrial beings, and the US government, in collusion with the other national powers of the Earth, is determined to keep this information from the general public. (Victor Marchetti, former Special Assistant to the Executive Director of the CIA, in an article for *Second Look* entitled 'How the CIA views the UFO Phenomenon', Vol 1, No 7, May 1979)

United Kingdom, 1988

The evidence that there are objects which have been seen in our atmosphere, and even on terra firma, that cannot be accounted for either as man-made objects or as any physical force or effect known to our scientists, seems to me to be overwhelming . . . A very large number of sightings have been vouched for by persons whose credentials seem to me unimpeachable. It is striking that so many have been trained observers, such as police officers and airline or military pilots. Their observations have in many instances ... been supported either by technical means such as radar or, even more convincingly, by ... interference with electrical apparatus of one sort or another ... (Lord Hill-Norton, Chief of Defence Staff, United Kingdom, 1973 and Chairman, Military Committee of NATO, 1974–7, in his foreword to Timothy Good's *Above Top Secret*)

Japan, 1990

First of all, I told a magazine this past January that, as an underdeveloped country with regards to the UFO problem, Japan had to take into account what should be done about the UFO question, and that we had to spend more time on these matters. In addition, I said that someone had to solve the UFO problem with far reaching vision at the same time. Secondly, I believe it is a reasonable time to take the UFO problem seriously as a reality ... I hope that this Symposium will contribute to peace on Earth from the point of view of outer space, and take the first step toward the international cooperation in the field of UFOs. (Toshiki Kaifu, Prime Minister of Japan in a letter to the Mayor of Hakui City, dated 24 June 1990, endorsing a forthcoming space and UFO symposium)

Belgium, 1991

In any case, the Air Force has arrived at the conclusion that a certain number of anomalous phenomena has been produced within Belgian airspace. The numerous testimonies of ground observations compiled in this book, reinforced by the reports of the night of 30–31 March [1990], have led us to face the hypothesis that a certain number of unauthorized aerial activities have taken place. Until now, not a single trace of aggressiveness has been signalled; military or civilian air traffic has not been perturbed nor threatened. We can therefore advance that the presumed activities do not constitute a direct menace.

The day will come undoubtedly when the phenomenon will be observed with technological means of detection and collection that will not leave a single doubt about its origin. This should lift a part of the veil that has covered the mystery for a long time. A mystery that continues to the present. But it exists, it is real, and that in itself is an important conclusion. (Major General Wilfred de Brouwer, Deputy Chief, Royal Belgian Air Force, in 'Postface' in *SOBEPS Vague d'OVNI sur la Belgique – Un Dossier Exceptionnel*, Brussels: SOBEPS, 1991)

Hungary, 1994

Around Szolnok many UFO reports have been received from the Ministry of Defence, which obviously and logically means that they [UFOs] know very well where they have to land and what they have to do. It is remarkable indeed that the Hungarian newspapers, in general newspapers everywhere, reject the reports of the authorities. (George Keleti, Minister of Defence, Hungary, in an article by Attila Lenart entitled 'Ask a Question of the Minister of Defence: George Keleti, Are You Afraid of a UFO Invasion?', *Nepszava*, Budapest, 18 August 1994)

6

CHANNELLING

Sightings of UFOs are concerned with identifying the vehicles – the hardware. Anybody looking at a number of different personal computers will gain very little information about the contents of each box, even less about the users and less still about the usage to which each computer is put, and next to nothing about the source or destination of each box.

Abduction stories have begun to provide some useful information. Hypnotic regression has given us some insight into the appearance and the actions of the inhabitants of some of the spacecraft. They appear to be breeding a new race of hybrid beings. For what purpose we do not know: whether it is for their benefit or ours, or whether the greys intend that the hybrids will inhabit our world or theirs. Furthermore, despite all the information gained via hypnotic regression, we are ultimately none the wiser about their goodwill, nor of that of any of the other alien races who are giving our planet the once-over.

Hypnotic regression of abduction victims only informs us about the greys from Zeta Reticuli, since they appear to be the only alien species performing abductions. We do not know whether it is they or another race that demonstrated their ultimate power by deactivating various US nuclear missile facilities from time to time – the missile launch control centre at Great Falls, Montana, in the spring of 1966, the missile centre at Malstrom Air Force Base in March 1967, and perhaps on a number of other occasions which have not become public knowledge.

The greys may in fact be a race of unmitigated liars, not dissimilar to many earth governments. They appear to be using people for genetic purposes, yet they claim to be here for our benefit, according to the messages they have given to numerous abductees. Bill Herrmann, who was abducted in March 1978 from near his home in Charleston, South Carolina, reports that his abductors informed him that they had tried to make contact with earth governments, but they had spurned their advances. It is hard to believe the good intentions of a race that subjects humans to genetic experiments; yet given their absolute technological superiority, they could have conquered the earth with consummate ease had their intentions been hostile.

WHAT IS CHANNELLING?

In this chapter I will examine channelling and the extent to which we are able to use it to learn more about UFOs and extraterrestrials. Channellers claim to receive messages from a variety of otherworldly sources, including the Archangel Gabriel, ascended masters and various ethereal, non-physical spirit 'energies' as well as extraterrestrial entities inhabiting specific planets in identifiable galaxies. One such entity is Bashar, who is channelled by Lyssa Royal and Darryl Anka. Bashar claims to be from the Essassani, a hybrid species – a genetic cross between humans and the little greys from Zeta Reticuli.

But does channelling represent an opportunity for us to learn, by direct communication, about the extraterrestrials and their intentions? Is it like a telephone link with alien races – possibly a short cut to finding out more about our alien visitors? Or is it the biggest fantasy of the new millennium? Are the channellers simply accessing a part of their own unconscious, without any link to other universes? Or could channelling even be a source of disinformation, with alien races using channellers to lull us into a state of false security about their true intentions?

What exactly is channelling? In *The Channeling Zone*, Michael Brown sees it as an expression of New Age irrationality:

Few expressions of New Age spirituality evoke greater skepticism and derision than does channeling, the practice of serving as a vessel for the voices of ancient or otherworldly beings. Channelers claim to be possessed by angels, aliens, and 'ascended masters' who speak through them, offering advice and solace. Intellectuals dismiss them as cranks and charlatans; evangelical Christians accuse them of trafficking with Satanic forces. Meanwhile, the steady spread of channeling from the West Coast to the American heartland fuels the fear that the United States now confronts an epidemic of public irrationality.

It is becoming more and more evident, however, that the stories of visitors from outer space are not just empty rumours, but reflect a reality, a reality that is being hidden from us by our various governments. It also exposes the lie that has been propagated by the Christian Church, that the human race is the only race of beings in the universe. The fact of extra-terrestrial visitors establishes absolutely in our minds that man is not the centre of the universe, and that we are not the most highly evolved beings.

In *Heaven on Earth: Dispatches from America's Spiritual Frontier* Michael D'Antonio estimates that some 40 million Americans are interested in New Age activities, 12 million of whom are active participants. The intellectual and scientific establishment condemns the growth of this movement as a disturbing 'epidemic' of anti-intellectual irrationality. Yet channelling clearly fulfils a need for authentic spiritual experience that many feel is denied by orthodox religion. The more orthodox in turn are dismissive of new forms of spiritual expression. Innovation invariably represents a threat to those in control of established practices, and they will inevitably feel compelled to defend the existing order, regardless of individual needs.

Many intellectuals, scientists and Christian leaders have endeavoured to find ways to denigrate and marginalize channelling as cranky, satanic and unscientific, and even though it might assist in providing useful additional information about extraterrestrials. Many ufologists see channelling as bedevilling the work of UFO research. In *Uninvited Guests*, Richard Hall, former Acting Director of the National Committee on Aerial

Phenomena, referred to contactee stories in the 1950s as emanating from 'a motley crew of psychic cooks and bottle washers'. The very irrationality of channelling represents a direct challenge to the establishment of Western society; and the Committee for the Scientific Investigation of Claims of the Paranormal (CSICOP) describes this irrationality as an 'apocalypse of unreason', heralding the emergence of a new Dark Age.

The limitations of Western science

Channellers and critics of the dominance of Western science see it as the expression of a male-oriented, male-centred, ethnocentric ideology. They see the price of the material benefits brought by Western science as a deadening and stultifying spiritual and intellectual stranglehold. While science purports to be objective, the commonly accepted lesson of quantum physics is the interrelationship between observer and observed – that the observer determines, by his or her very assumptions, the nature of what is observed.

Science points to its seemingly absolute dominance of nature, but ignores its impotence in the face of nature's forces such as volcanoes, earthquakes and tornadoes. Similarly it purports to hold the keys to ultimate objective knowledge and reality, but ignores the unquestioned assumptions at its core. It uses rational and conceptual tools to determine the nature of what it observes, but it fails completely to enable us to understand human emotions and feelings. It only enables us to understand human beings at a superficial level, and fails to give credence to the thirst for the otherworldly and for the mystery of life.

Science is clearly only a partial tool, useful for the development of technology and the creation of human comfort, but a charlatan when it tries to be the ruling ideology of our times. A scientific view of the world is bankrupt in appreciating or understanding the non-material, whether it is human emotions or communications from distant extraterrestrial intelligence. Phenomena which are beyond the purview of scientists' ability to explain, are dumped into a special category called 'paranormal'.

The very need to create such a category suggests that science holds centre stage in determining what is normality and deciding that all else is abnormal. It is a form of intellectual trickery that makes a mockery of almost everything that is human. The term 'paranormal' also indicates the failure of science by indicating that which it cannot explain. Science is a mighty god that has served us well; but the time has now come to put it in its place and to begin to see its limitations.

It must also be acknowledged that science has led the human race to the brink of atomic extinction and potential annihilation from pollution. Most New Age adherents challenge the one-dimensional way in which science has skewed human development to focus almost exclusively on the material. It encourages disconnection and disparateness, self-determining in its conclusions. By contrast, channellers and their sources see the universe as a unified interconnected field.

> Quantum physics has been exploring the idea that the observer and the observed are part of the same one thing. We do not exist within a random, unconnected universe, but within a rich tapestry where all pieces are interwoven together. (Lyssa Royal and Keith Priest, *Preparing for Contact*)

Is channelling becoming a new religion?

Interconnected spirituality is not just a sudden spontaneous outburst against a constraining structurally oriented ideology. It can in fact trace its roots back to Native American spirituality and beyond, to many other native peoples who have managed to retain the remnants of their pre-scientific practices.

Traditional religion is seen as just as deadening in its effects as science. It is preoccupied with empty rituals, inflexible rules, power struggles, dogma and doctrine. In *The Channeling Zone* Michael Brown summarizes the channelling view of traditional religion as follows:

> Not only do religions fail to offer authentic spirituality . . . they

are obsolete vestiges of an earlier historical era . . . Religions are spiritual movements that stopped moving . . . the major problem with formal religions is their alleged obsession with hierarchy and control.

Channelling, by contrast, is non-hierarchical, non-authoritarian and genderless. It provides participants with metaphysical, spiritual, intellectual and emotional tools that enable individual people to tap into their own divinity. While channellers are receiving communications from their source, they are linked into a part of themselves. They appear to be passive recipients, like a radio receiver, transmitting the received signal, but an examination of the messages shows that the neurological structure of the human host is used by the distant spirit and plays a part in the communication. This is shown in the way that the channeller often uses terminology which, one imagines, would be unknown to a spirit being that has never visited earth society.

CHANNELLERS AND THEIR SOURCES

The Seth material

In your system of reality you are learning what mental energy is, and how to use it. You do this by constantly transforming your thoughts and emotions into physical form. You are supposed to get a clear picture of your inner development by perceiving the exterior environment. What seems to be a perception, an objective concrete event independent from you, is instead the materialization of your own inner emotions, energy and mental environment. (Dictated by Seth to Jane Roberts, *The Seth Material*)

Jane Roberts, who died in 1984, channelled the Seth material. She was one of our best known channels, and the Seth material is well known. Using material from almost 2,000 sessions over 20 years she and her husband, Robert Butts, have produced 23 books already, with another 17 manuscripts not yet published.

The Seth material challenges the very fabric of accepted global thought from which most theories and conclusions are presently drawn, especially the 'law' of cause and effect. According to Seth, we are given the gift of the gods – the gift of creativity. He says there is only one rule of physical existence, and that is the fact that we literally create our individual realities through our thoughts, attitudes and beliefs. Events don't happen to us; we cause them by what we expect to see in our world and our lives. Every event we encounter and participate in is a physical reflection of what we think and feel. The implications of this statement are startling, for if we have created the reality of our individual and global lives, then surely we can change what we don't like. (Lynda Dahl, *Ten Thousand Whispers: A Guide to Conscious Creation*, 1995)

Barbara Marciniak, who has also received Seth material, provides significant in-depth metaphysical insights. A Connecticut woman, Frances Morse, claims to have encountered Seth during a near-death experience in 1975. Seth is in fact a generic name used by an extraterrestrial collective intelligence which channels through a number of different people.

Lyssa Royal's three friends

Most channelled entities do not clearly identify themselves as extraterrestrial. Lyssa Royal is the exception rather than the rule in that she channels identifiable extraterrestrial sources. She describes the process in the following way:

I put myself into a meditative state in which my personality disconnects from my normal perception of reality. Another consciousness (or entity) links energetically and telepathically with my brain and then uses it as a translation device for the concepts discussed. In no way am I 'taken over' by another entity. It is entirely a cooperative process between myself and the entity. It can be discontinued at any time by my choice. When the session is completed, I retain only a dreamlike memory of what has transpired. (Lyssa Royal and Keith Priest, *Preparing for Contact: A Metamorphosis of Consciousness*)

Lyssa Loyal channels Sasha, Germane and Bashar. Sasha is a female from the Pleiades star group. In *The Pleiadian Agenda*, Barbara Hand Clow writes about information that is channelled from Satya, director of a group of Pleiadians and

Keeper of the Records on Alcyone, the central star of the Pleiades.

Germane is a non-physical group consciousness that often channels about extraterrestrial history, whereas Bashar is a male of the Essassani species. The Essassani are a genetic cross between humans and Zeta Reticuli visitors – the little greys who have been carrying out the abductions that have caused such distress and misery to so many abductees. Betty Hill's abductors claimed Zeta Reticuli as their home base.

WHAT CHANNELLING TELLS US

Reasons for making contact

Channelling represents a source of information and contact with extraterrestrials not otherwise available to us. Ufologists who believe in scientifically determined physical reality as the predominant reality, as opposed to any kind of spirit-based reality, are concerned primarily with spacecraft and metallic objects – chasing the getaway car, as Budd Hopkins so aptly put it. Channellers by contrast provide a ready access to the occupants of the spacecraft insofar as they receive direct communications from extraterrestrial sources – by spiritual mobile phone, as it were.

While the abduction phenomenon demonstrates our total impotence against the power of the extraterrestrials to whisk people away at their whim, the channellers provide some sense of what is going on. Extraterrestrials have apparently been visiting the earth since the beginning of time. They speak about our prehistory, when extraterrestrials visited the earth in great numbers and assisted in the construction of the great crystal which was the power source for the entire civilization of Atlantis.

Modern man is a recent phase in the history of the earth – a greenfield-site innovation, and way behind most other civilizations in our technological and spiritual development. None the less the code of extraterrestrial basic law is never to interfere unless asked to help. Why, in that case, one wonders, are the little greys intervening now? Do they not know the rules of extraterrestrial 'good practice'?

According to Lyssa Royal in *ET Civilizations*, the greys, or Zeta Reticuli, were a civilization similar to ours who unwittingly chose a path of self-destruction which resulted in a genetic crisis. One of their biggest mistakes was to breed out feelings. They were only just able to prevent themselves from being completely wiped out, and became sterile as a consequence. They are now endeavouring to acquire human genetic material in order to regenerate themselves. They specifically want material from a race that carries the code derived from one of the original extraterrestrial races, the Vegans. This code is said to exist still in human beings, into whom it was bred eons ago, from both the Vegans and the Lyrans, the first group to incarnate and take on physical form.

Another reason given by a number of channellers for the increase in the number of sightings in recent years is a heightening of our collective consciousness. Apart from the greys, who have their own agenda, other extraterrestrials who are aware of the impending transformation are keen to assist humanity to move into a new age. Many of earth's great advances in the past are said to have been achieved with the assistance of extraterrestrial help.

Although many extraterrestrials have a humanoid appearance, this is by no means the only shape that they adopt when they take physical form. Humanity is in fact one of the least developed of the intelligent life forms in the universe. The exceedingly primitive and warlike nature of man is one of the principal reasons that extraterrestrial visitors have not been more open in the past. They see that mankind has been challenged by the notion of intelligent life elsewhere in the universe and has not been ready to adjust, although this is now changing. As Lyssa Royal says in *ET Civilizations*:

> When a planet is getting ready for extraterrestrial contact and contact with new levels of reality, the brains of the species on the planet begin evolving rapidly. This is happening right now on Earth. As the brains begin evolving to another level, a new sub-species begins to happen, the brain-wave capacity of the human

changes, and therefore their ability to perceive other levels of reality begins changing. It is then they realize the extraterrestrials are not going to suddenly appear to humans; rather, humans will begin to perceive the ET contact which has gone on all along.

This is how Sasha, a Pleiadian who channels through Lyssa Royal, describes making contact with extraterrestrial races. She sees it as a two-way process, not a passive one in which humans behave as a non-participating audience.

What the alien races are like

The suggestion that human beings are descended from the apes has always been surmise and conjecture. Although it has served as a useful hypothesis, no evidence has ever been presented to prove it beyond any reasonable doubt. And the story of the creation as told in the Bible sounds closer to mythology than firm evidence about the origin of man. So the idea that we may be descended from extraterrestrials who once visited the earth is no less convincing than the ape hypothesis or biblical mythology. For many, it is the most credible of the three ideas, and deserves at the very least to have parity with the other two beliefs about the origin of mankind.

Germane is a non-physical group consciousness channelled by Lyssa Royal, who describes humans as descended primarily from Lyrans, but also from Vegans. Many people may be puzzled by the description of Germane as a 'non-physical group consciousness'. In order to understand this expression, we need to recognize the predominant belief in our culture that material precedes essence. It is symptomatic, as I have said before, of the absolute dominance of scientific materialism over our value system, to the extent that most of us have come to believe that it is the natural order of things, and the only way to think about our life and the universe.

We tend to see things spiritual as a by-product of our physical existence. But the channellers and most spiritually oriented people see the material as an expression of the spiritual. Extraterrestrial entities are primarily spiritual energies, some of whom have taken material form and some of whom have chosen to remain as spirit, intelligence, consciousness, or energy – the words are to some extent interchangeable. In the case of Germane, this is not a single intelligence, but a collective intelligence that has not taken physical form.

According to Germane, the Lyrans have evolved on different planets into a number of subgroups – giants, redheads, Caucasians, dark-skinned Lyrans, bird-like Lyrans, cat-like Lyrans, and Pleiadians. The giants are between 6 and 9 feet tall, and are the group primarily responsible for the ancient legends about gods in mythology and the Bible. The redheads have strawberry blond hair and green eyes. They are the pioneers of new worlds with a marauding temperament which has been weakened by their merging with the Pleiadians, who are a non-volatile and non-violent race.

The Caucasian Lyrans comprise the group from which many of the earth's inhabitants have sprung. The dark-skinned Lyrans had a powerful influence on the inhabitants of the Indian sub-continent. Their initial temperament was one of extreme peacefulness. Reference to this group of visitors can be found in some Sanskrit literature.

The bird-like Lyrans look very thin and frail, with angular, sharp faces and bird-like eyes. They are unemotional and intellectual entities, primarily scientists, explorers and philosophers, who spend most of their time travelling and visiting other worlds. As a consequence they have minimal involvement with intergalactic politics.

The cat-like types are not cat people but humanoids with feline qualities. They are agile, and strong, with a cat-like nose and a small delicate mouth. They have a peach-coloured fuzz, rather than fur, to protect their skin from the harsh ultraviolet radiation on their indigenous planet.

The Pleiadians are a Lyran splinter group, some of whom went directly to the Pleiades while others spent time on earth where they mixed their genes with the locals. They range in height from 5 to almost 7 feet in height, in hair colouring from blond to dark haired, and their eyes from light blue to light brown. They are more like earth humans than any other extra-terrestrial group, but have a very different perception of reality.

The Vegans are less varied in appearance than the Lyrans from whom they are descended. They consist of the Reptilians, the Sirians, the Pleiadians, the Orion civilization and the Zeta Reticuli. The primary subgroup is a dark-skinned humanoid, with a tough durable skin with many more layers than humans have. Their hair is dark, sometimes with a greenish tinge, although some groups have no hair at all. It is quite likely that very dark Indians and Africans are descended from this group. Their eyes have very large, dark pupils and irises which are particularly striking because of the contrast with the whites of the eyes.

A Vegan group with a non-human appearance is the Reptilians, who have a green tinge because of the copper base in the skin and the blood. Although this type is mammalian, the small nose and downward thrust of the jaw create a non-human appearance. The Sirians are characterized by their large, angled eyes. It is said that the earth's dolphins and whales are expressions of Sirian consciousness.

The Orions are a civilization of a few billion beings. They are Vegan mainstream in origin with a few Reptilians in the Orion group of stars. All have bodies and skins which are lubricated with a fatty, oil substance. The colour of the eyes of some of the priests can become bright blue.

As we have seen throughout this book, the Zeta Reticuli are generally referred to as little greys. They are much shorter than the other extraterrestrial races – typically 3 feet 5 inches to 4 feet 6 inches in height, but occasionally 5 feet. Their short stature and peculiar appearance in having a very large head in relation to the rest of the body, and large eyes without eyelids, is due to a genetic malfunction which almost resulted in their extinction; their current appearance is the result of the genetic engineering they underwent in order to survive as a race.

Their purpose in visiting earth is to reintroduce back into their race the original Lyran genetic codes, which are stored in human genes. Human beings are able to provide them with a kind of two-for-one deal in that we carry a mixture of both Lyran and Vegan DNA codes. Earth is a biological treasure chest for the Zeta Reticuli, although it is not, according to Germane, the one-way trade that it may initially appear to be.

Human society is benefiting from the activities of the greys, but he did not specify how.

The significance of this description is that it is similar to the descriptions given by almost all abductees of the appearance of their abductors. It also relates to the descriptions provided by the US government in two secret documents: the briefing paper for President-Elect Eisenhower in November 1952 (*see* chapter 5) and the MJ-12 Special Operations Manual of April 1954, published by Stanton Friedman in *Top Secret/Majic* (*see* chapter 3).

All of these extraterrestrial races have been mentioned by other channellers. They have also reported the existence of many other races, too numerous and diverse to list here. My purpose in describing some of the races is to underline something that we are all instinctively aware of – that we not alone in the universe.

THE PLEIADIANS AND BILLY MEIER

Edouard 'Billy' Meier, a 60-year-old man who lives near Zurich, Switzerland, claims to have channelled Semjase, a female resident of the planet Erra in the area of Alcyone, a star in the Pleiadian region. He has had multiple contacts with extraterrestrials since the age of five. He was contacted while he was a child by Sfath, an elderly Pleiadian male who took him aboard a pear-shaped craft. Sfath handed Meier over to Asket, a female who described her race as a closely linked to the Pleiadians. She communicated phenomenal information over the years. Asket has also communicated with Edward White, a South African electrician. Billy Meier supports his account with hundreds of incredible photos and many 8mm videos of the Pleiadian space vehicles that visited him by arrangement, one of which can be clearly seen 'parked' in his driveway.

Meier's story, like that of many channellers, sounds incredible and truly stretches the mind of the uninitiated. It should be recognized, however, that for people whose reality is determined primarily by the media, it must be difficult to deal with material that has not been 'officially' sanctioned. How often have ufologists heard the words, 'Well, if it's real, how come I haven't seen it on the television or heard it on the radio, or read about in a newspaper?' Of course this response in no way challenges the reality of the work of the channellers. It is somewhat like proving the existence of God – we do not know, but it is a good idea to keep an open mind on the subject.

Billy Meier has produced detailed diagrams of Pleiadian beamships and other spacecraft. These are further substantiated by photographs of UFOs 'visiting' his home in Switzerland in 1977, one of which is described as

... a circular disk-shaped craft with a high cupulo on top sitting about 1 meter above the ground on a very coherent straight-sided beam of white light. The disk-shaped lower part of the strange craft was of a bright matt silver color and was rotating slowly in a counterclockwise direction. The rim, or edge, of the disk about 60 cm thick, was squared off into vertical sides which seemed to consist of myriads of small flapper vanes mounted vertically, and which moved from right to left and back again through a 90 degree arc in a rhythmic sequence. A 3 meter diameter underflange of the base of the craft projected down about 20 cm below the lower disk surface and was also squared off on the sides. The intense white light which seemed to support the ship was projected down vertically from this lower flange. Inside of the intense white light Meier could see a cantilever stair of 5 steps descending from the lower center of the craft to the ground surface.

Back to the rim, he could see that as it rotated slowly and the vertical flapper vanes moved back and forth, an aura of rainbow colors was thrown off to the sides around the rim. The 7 meter diameter main disk structure was about 1.5 meters measured from top to bottom, and the lower surface showed more of a curve than the upper.

On top of that a 2.5 meter diameter cupulo with 1 meter vertical sides having 8 bulging hemispherical windows set into them, rose to a 70 cm thick rolled static ring having about the same 3 meter diameter as the bottom underflange of the base. This part was a luminous orange color and a bright yellow-white light shown from the 'windows'. The top of this cupulo structure blended into a smooth curved dome of some kind of colored dark glass. It looked like glass and has a smooth finish but he could not see any reflections in its surface. (Wendelle Stevens, *UFO Contact from the Pleiades*)

The photographs show the craft flying over Meier's house and 'parked' in his driveway. If it is a hoax, it is certainly very elaborate and expensive.

His Pleiadian contacts told him about the earth's early history and physical life on Hyperboria, the continent that encompassed all of the land mass at that time, and the story of the pre-human civilizations of Lemuria and Atlantis. He is also able to provide a wealth of information about extra-terrestrials and their civilization, and about their activities on earth.

7

SPIRITUAL DIMENSIONS

Are we human beings having a spiritual experience, or spiritual beings having a human experience? Are the extraterrestrial visitors physical beings similar to ourselves? Or are they beings who have developed over the eons into something more spiritual than us?

SPIRITUAL ENERGY

The spiritual view is that everything that exists is an expression of spiritual energy in material form, in that specific configuration at that time. All spirit is energy vibrating at a particular frequency, and each vibrating frequency – or 'vibration' – can be referred to as a dimension. Human beings in this schema are third-dimension vibrations or third-dimensional beings, beings existing on the third dimension.

New Age people use a variety of different expressions to express the view that mankind is on the verge of moving into a fourth-dimension consciousness. In other words, as we develop our intuitive and spiritual qualities, we begin to vibrate at a higher frequency, which gives us access to information that we cannot obtain while remaining at the third-dimension. One could also say that our consciousness is being raised, possibly by outside forces, rather than a development that is under our conscious control. New Age people generally believe that we do play a role in facilitating the process of enhancing our consciousness or vibration.

In becoming fourth-dimensional beings, we become

increasingly able to see and experience ET visitors. Channellers are said to communicate by putting their third-dimension ego into abeyance. They access a higher dimensional state via their unconscious, which enables them to communicate across the ether with different kinds of energies or intelligences.

Many extraterrestrials beings exist in the fourth and fifth dimensions, which enables them to appear and be seen by us at the third dimension and then disappear from view in a split second, back to their regular dimension. There is a suggestion that their higher vibrational state also enables them to eavesdrop on our thoughts, feelings and conversations, of which there is ample evidence in ufological literature. Because of their higher-frequency development they can, moreover, send powerful suggestive messages to people, who may find themselves walking or driving to a particular spot from where they are whisked aboard a waiting craft.

With reference to the greys, I believe it is also possible that their ability to eavesdrop may be the result of superior technology, rather than their higher spiritual development. They have been described by more than one channelled extraterrestrial source as being only a step further along in their development than ourselves. So if we are infants in the extraterrestrial universe, the greys are children.

Intelligences that vibrate at the sixth and particularly the seventh dimensions do not take a physical form, thus Germane, who is channelled by Lyssa Royal, is a non-physical group intelligence or consciousness. We would be unable to see energies that vibrate at these dimensions, although those of us who are more attuned may well be able to sense their presence. Channellers have developed the ability to receive communications from these higher-dimensional energies. Humans may prefer to think of them as 'beings' although they are not beings in the conventional sense. It would be easier for us to understand if we take the view that we are primarily energies expressed in material form as a humanoid body – the Adam Kadmon body, as it is called by spiritual writers.

The opposite view of reality, the scientific material view, which predominates in the Western world is that spirit is an attribute of body. Scientific materialism is so inadequate at explaining the non-material that even the straightforward fact of ghosts being trapped spirits becomes a mystery. Many other phenomena regarded as paranormal become relatively easily understandable once we give up the idea that science can explain everything, including the non-material.

BELIEF

Is God the creator a spirit energy vibrating at the highest level, or is God the source of all other vibrations? My understanding is that God is the divine energy from which all other energies are derived, somewhat like a spring from which all waters flow. Each drop is separate and yet interlinked in a contiguous whole. Each extraterrestrial energy that communicates with a human can be likened to a collection of drops that have taken on their own consciousness, separate from the water flowing around them, and yet part of the grand flow.

Many New Age and religious people might well regard my third-dimension description of this aspect of spirituality as sacrilegious. Friends who are more spiritually oriented than me have been at pains to explain that fourth-dimensional consciousness is a state that can only be experienced and not understood. Others have said that it is accessed via the heart and not the intellect and that it should not, therefore, be written about in a matter-of-fact way.

One of the misunderstandings that may arise from my earth-bound exposition of life as the expression of a spiritual energy source is that it suggests that other spirit energies have an existence that is independent and separate from us. This is not so. All spirit energy is closely interlinked. In a sense if we do not believe that other energies are there, we cannot experience them. This view echoes the Christian concept of faith.

When we access our higher-dimensional consciousness we become able to see other spirit energies subsisting at that vibration. In order to experience at a higher dimension, it is essential that we believe it is possible, in the same way that is highly unlikely someone who does not believe that he can run a mile in four minutes will be able to do so. It does not mean that everyone who believes they can do so will necessarily be able to, but belief is a precondition. I suggest that the very act of believing has a role in altering our vibration.

Access to higher-dimensional communications is therefore determined by our own actions. If you do not knock you will not be heard. If you do not tune in to the appropriate frequency on a radio, you will not hear the radio station you want. Channellers appear to make themselves available to whatever random intelligence chooses to communicate through them. It seems unselective, and I do not have a view about why an intelligence chooses a given channeller.

Regardless of who chooses whom in this realm of celestial communications, I submit that our spiritual development is a precondition of communications with extraterrestrial intelligences, and that they will continue to taunt us, always staying just out of reach, until we satisfy them that we are ready to communicate. Given the neurotic behaviour of mankind and the warlike actions of governments, I would remain at a distance if I were a highly evolved extraterrestrial until I felt that it was safe to make contact.

Sasha, the Pleiadian female who communicates via Lyssa Royal has made the suggestion that when humankind has 'a rich inner life, you will attract us more strongly than you could ever do now by looking in the sky instead of within'. Carl Jung made the observation that even though UFOs have an independent physical reality, he thought that they were a product of the unconscious – which sounds contradictory. I suggest that the link between our inner processes and extraterrestrial contact is that the visitors have a way of knowing when certain people are ready to make contact. It is a 'correspondent' relationship.

The little greys are an exception, however, in that they appear to break the rules of extraterrestrial etiquette. They abduct people against their will and without adequate explanation. They seem little better than earth governments in the way they enforce their will on people. Perhaps their behaviour can be accounted for by their lack of spiritual development, being only marginally more evolved than ourselves. And having made a mess of their own genetic inheritance, they are making us unwilling participants in a desperate bid to regenerate their race – without any concern for our feelings.

THE KEYS OF ENOCH

One of the clues to a spiritual extra-dimensional understanding of alien spacecraft may be contained in the book *The Keys of Enoch*. The original Book of Enoch is an ancient text composed before the birth of Christ, and written in great epic style. The archangel Uriel reveals to the prophet Enoch the secrets of the 'workings of heaven, earth and the seas, and all the elements'.

Although it was considered a sacred text, and referred to in other texts, it was not in fact included in the Bible. In addition to the original Aramaic document, there are known to have been several versions of the text including Slavonic and Ethiopic copies. In the 18th century the Scottish explorer James Bruce found copies in Ethiopia.

Fragments of the original Aramaic version were discovered in the 1950s in one of 11 caves on the north-western shore of the Dead Sea, together with 400 other ancient manuscripts, including a complete copy of the Hebrew Old Testament. The Book of Enoch is fascinating as an historical document, but the arcane wisdom which it attempts to reveal to mankind is sadly somewhat obscure. *The Keys of Enoch: The Book of Knowledge* may provide some insight into its meaning.

It is a spiritual scientific textbook that examines the greatest mysteries of our time, including the biggest conundrum – why we exist. The information was not channelled, but given to the author, J J Hurtak on 2 and 3 January 1973 in a remarkable revelation. It is intended to be used to facilitate mankind's next great step in spiritual evolution.

While Dr Hurtak was at prayer, asking God about the meaning of life, his room was filled with light and Master Ophanim Enoch appeared to him. He conveyed Hurtak into the Merak and Muscida region of stars, where he was informed that the earth is controlled by powers that inhabit the Ursa Major group of stars. They control the gateway between earth and the higher heavens.

The text is a cosmological blueprint for man's evolution to a higher state of consciousness. It provides a link between scientific and spiritual solutions, to facilitate a quantum leap in man's evolution. Embedded in the text may well be a clue about the feasibility of space travel.

The technique of space travel

Dr Hurtak was shown how the higher intelligences travel through space by the gravitational modulation of light waves. He goes on to describe, in technical language, the process by which these higher intelligences enter a planet's atmosphere. He writes about 'measuring the magnetic parameters of the planetary event horizon' and 'rotational circumversion' of two conical sections of light being brought together. He goes on to describe how 'by connecting their relativity with a given planetary relativity' space vehicles 'put a spiral of light within a spiral of light which allows them to connect with levels of three-dimensional space from the standpoint of expanding and contracting gravitational density'.

Not being a scientist, I am unable to comment on the language he uses, nor have I read any scientific appraisal of this text. Dr Hurtak he explains that the reason why some space-craft appear to have a form of stealth technology is that they come from a higher coding of light, which I understand as a higher vibration. This enables them to enter our three-dimensional world via a multidimensional hole and travel in wavelengths which are higher than those which we can see. This is is somewhat like our inability to hear a dog whistle because it vibrates at a pitch that is higher than our audio range. These spacecraft are able to move faster than the speed of light and travel via time tunnels or wormholes as they search out new worlds. By deliberately slowing down their frequency, they are able to make themselves visible to the inhabitants of a given world. They 'materialize within the molecular frequency of the given spectrum of light energy'.

The mystery of triangular flight patterns

The triangular pattern in which many extraterrestrial craft fly has long puzzled observers. When abductees such as Bill Herrmann, who was picked up near his home in Charleston, South Carolina, in March 1978, asked about this strange manner of flying, they were told that it is because the radar from nearby military installations interfered with their navigational systems. It is even rumoured to be a reason why one of the extraterrestrial craft crashed.

According to Dr Hurtak, 'The Higher Evolution has flight patterns which go through multiple tracings of light, through complicated triangular coordinates. They do this to key into certain time periods of the species' growth and development.' Space vehicles are often seen as three craft flying in triangular formation. They do this to balance each other when 'entering and leaving the electromagnetic and gravitational density of the planets'.

Transvirulence

Dr Hurtak refers to the method by which a light energy field is placed around a human and projected into a space vehicle as 'transvirulence'. The human is floated aboard a spacecraft via a 'float vacuum' into a central module. During his or her time aboard the space vehicle, the human is 'biochemically respatialized' in order to be able to exist at the wavelength of the creatures aboard the craft.

This throws additional light on the inability of many people to recall their time aboard the craft. It has been suggested that this is because they have been instructed by their captors that they would forget their experience. However, hypnotic regression has revealed that, more recently, some people have not been given this instruction, yet they are still unable to recall their experience consciously. Many, however, report having felt tired and disoriented. 'There is less of the gross material "you" in the physical geometry of what is "your body", but it is "you" in the transfigured matter–energy form within the chemistry and geometry of what is considered necessary for communion with you', according to Dr Hurtak.

Enoch showed Dr Hurtak an effect that has been noticed by quantum physicists, namely, the extent to which an object can be changed by the projected 'thought-form energy packet' of the observer. He describes how a 'radical change takes place in the reality mass because of the perceptual mass interacting with thought-forms'. By modulating our brain signals as we project our thoughts, we should be able to communicate instantaneously without any of the time lag associated with words.

UFOs as spiritual entities

Scientists are concerned with the study of phenomena that can be observed, measured and tested. This is a mechanistic view of life, and yet it is apparent that we are more than machines. Quantum physics is clear about the extent to which the observer alters the nature of what he observes, but also, by implication, the extent to which we determine much of our personal reality by our consciousness, energy and intention.

By regarding UFOs as exclusively physical phenomena, we limit ourselves to UFO-spotting, without ever learning about the occupants of the craft. Such a view precludes us from understanding the possiblity that UFOs and their occupants are anything other than physical and material.

8

THE NATURE OF REALITY

THE ALIEN PHENOMENON IS BOTH TANGIBLE AND INTANGIBLE

In this book I have endeavoured to show that UFOs exist, that they are real, tangible, metallic objects that can be seen and touched, and that the occupants of some of them really are removing people from earth for varying periods of time and performing unpleasant experiments upon their bodies. I have also suggested that it is a mistake to see spacecraft and their occupants only in terms of the tangible.

But we are faced with an extraterrestrial phenomenon that has a strong intangible element to it. Channellers show us that it is possible to communicate with the occupants of spacecraft, or at least with people who form part of the communities from which they come. They provide us with a useful way of gleaning knowledge about our visitors, not just knowledge about their nature, but also about their society and its background, and even possibly about their technology.

Dr Hurtak, who is specific about not being a channeller but whose information is derived from a non-terrestrial source, Master Ophanim Enoch, writes about extraterrestrial technology, although the scientific detail is beyond my understanding. He demonstrates and confirms the feasibility of acquiring information about other universes, extraterrestrial races and their technology by a means other than scientific laboratory work.

Channelling in general has long been regarded as an arcane and mysterious practice, an arena in which cranks and charlatans abound. The arbitrary harshness of these judgements, I submit, is itself suspect. It is difficult to measure the validity of information about another society and culture of which we have no direct first-hand knowledge. Would we have believed the stories of Marco Polo, in the late 13th century, about the great wealth and sophistication of China – a civilization more developed than his own? Would we have believed him had we been fellow citizens of his native Venice? Even today, in a recent publication, he has been slated as a liar and fraud who never set foot in China, and his story has been lambasted as a tale made up from rumours and stories from other travellers. Similarly, I wonder how could we today establish the veracity of information acquired via channellers about advanced civilizations that exist in outer space, millions of miles away.

Channelling uses the unconscious mind as a means of communication. In reading some channelled texts, I am puzzled about the link between the communication and the channeller's own value system. It would be useful to be able to minimize the channeller's own 'spin', in the same way that when we listen to somebody's account of a conversation, we usually try to get our own 'feel' for what was said. Like the rest of us, channellers all have their idiosyncrasies, and their pet notions, which are clearly discernable from time to time in the messages that they are relaying. Nevertheless, despite any unconscious distortion by the channeller, receiving communications from extraterrestrial sources is an amazingly useful means of receiving extraterrestrial communications – like having a celestial telephone via which we can speak to entities in the very heart of other distant worlds. Perhaps we should be rehearsing those questions we need to ask them in order to build up a compendium of information about their worlds. It would seem to me to be a more useful, even if still somewhat suspect, means of acquiring information about UFOs and their occupants than concentrating exclusively on UFO-spotting.

SCIENTIFIC IDEOLOGY AND SPRIRITUAL DEVELOPMENT

The over-dominance of the culture of what I refer to as scientific materialism has become stifling. It is an ideology that is becoming reactionary and a barrier to further human spiritual development. And spiritual development is the very route that we need to take if we are to learn more about our extraterrestrial visitors. It is the means by which we can treat with them on an equal footing. At present, by all accounts, we are the savages in the unfolding extraterrestrial drama.

I am not by any means decrying science or denying the huge debt that we owe to it. The very fact that I am entering these words on my 166Mhz Pentium computer and can transmit them directly to my publisher is a miracle of modern science. But although I am not opposed to science or technological development, I abhor is the protective ideology in which scientists and their acolytes cloak themselves in the belief that their grasp of ultimate reality is as it were divinely inspired, simply because they currently hold the intellectual high ground. The fear expressed by some scientists, that with the spread of New Age ideas we are in danger of embarking on a new era of darkness, is ill founded and overdramatic.

Every movement seems to gather around itself an intellectual support structure and belief system – in effect, an ideology. The recently collapsed centrally planned or command economies of Eastern Europe could not have existed without a belief in a Marxist or communist ideology. Similarly, the so-called capitalist or market-based mode of economic organization is supported by a belief in liberal democracy and a degree of individual freedom of choice. Both the economic and the political belief system are concerned with the most effective way to organize the material aspect of our lives. The current mode in which this is organized has enabled us to conquer nature, to the extent that nature can be conquered, and to control our environment, from my central heating to my personal computer and the electricity that makes both possible. These are a products of scientific discovery, which is concerned with the understanding and conquest of nature and the harnessing of natural forces.

This quest takes up a significant portion of the lives of many brilliant and remarkable people. It also commands often huge material resources from the state and from private enterprise, resources which have to be bid for in competition with other contenders, such as social services, health, the military etc. Arguments need to be marshalled to justify the expenditure, and in the process assumptions are foisted upon the listeners to mobilize their thinking in a particular direction – and ideology is the means by which we mobilize people's opinions. Ideology is the governing assumption which is implicit in the argument. It is the screen through which we see the world around us – usually without seeing the screen itself.

Scientific materialism is the view that the world is composed primarily of matter – matter that can be measured and tested. It devalues realities and ways of looking at the world which are not principally materially based, such as psychic phenomena and spiritual experience. What it cannot explain it denigrates. It represents a tyranny of rationality and analytical reason. It regards itself as the primary arbiter of what is real and what is acceptable. Psychics and people who have had profound spiritual experiences are often dismissed as crazy and crackpot. Yet those of us who have such experiences know that they are real, whether they are extraterrestrial abductions or channelled communications.

Those who make these criticisms represent the ideology of a movement which has brought us to the very brink of global annihilation, and the potential destruction of our environment by pollution. A more spiritually based value system that is more in touch with most people's inner requirements and more caring for the environment that supports us, does not herald a new dark age. By contrast, it is a more balanced way of looking at the world.

Furthermore, we will learn more about the strange and arresting phenomena that are assailing our skies by adopting a less materially based and more spiritually oriented approach than the one-dimensional UFO-spotting approach adopted by many ufologists. As Arthur C Clarke once said, 'Any sufficiently advanced technology is indistinguishable from magic.'

One example of the need for a different approach is the

Merkabah, referred to in *The Keys of Enoch* as a 'vehicle of light'. It is not clear whether it refers to a spacecraft or to an energy field that can be used for astral journeys, but Drunvalo Melchizedek, who conducts training courses on the subject, describes it as a vehicle for ascension and also as a thought-form consciousness – a crystalline energy field that expands in specific geometrical shapes around the body. It is a means by which we can access our fourth-dimension consciousness by following a particular pattern of focused breathing.

Once the Merkabah is generated as a counter-rotating field of light, it adopts a shape that is remarkably similar to the traditional 'flying saucer' shape. Once generated, it can transport the spirit and the body from one dimension, or world, to another. Inter-dimensional travel involves counter-rotating energy fields, or vortices, described in the Bible as whirlwinds – 'Behold, he [Yahweh] shall come up as clouds, and his chariots shall be as a whirlwind' (Jeremiah 4:13), and 'Behold, the Lord rideth upon a swift cloud' (Isaiah 19:1).

Many witnesses describe alien craft as having a rotating band of light spinning in an anticlockwise direction about the middle section. The rotation is reported to slow down as the craft approaches closer to the earth. The relationship between extra-terrestrial spacecraft as clearly visible metallic objects and the description of extraterrestrials as manifestations of a particular frequency vibration is a puzzling contrast. Given our conventional view of the world as a physical, tangible thing, many people are likely to find this juxtaposition of the material and the spiritual difficult to accept.

UFOs are often described as performing a 90 degree turn before disappearing. This is a typical example, according to Drunvalo Melchizedek, of the occupants of the craft harmonizing their consciousness and, *through linked breathing*, disappearing into another dimension or world. The different dimensions are not necessarily removed in space – they are all present at the same time, in the room in which you have been reading these words.

APPENDICES

UFO ORGANIZATIONS

INTERNATIONAL

MUFON – The Mutual UFO Network
103 Oldtowne Road
Seguin, TX 78155–4099
Tel: 210–379–9216
web: www.rutgers.edu/~mcgrew/mufon/
The world's largest UFO organization was set up in 1969. It describes itself as a grass-roots organization in that the leadership and motivation comes from the local level. In North America, each region has a state or provincial director who oversees the investigative activities of the field investigators. An international co-ordinator and seven continental co-ordinators work with foreign representatives and national directors in a number of countries. MUFON is no lightweight organization. It has a board of 21 directors, an executive committee that manages the organization and an extensive team of consultants, most of whom are MAs or PhDs drawn from a variety of fields. The organization publishes a monthly magazine, has an Internet page, organizes international conferences and provides field investigators with a manual.

The following are the telephone numbers of MUFON offices in North America.

Alabama
Lavada S Pitts, Assistant State Director, (205) 533–7321

Alaska
Norman L Mark, State Director, (907) 337–9499

Arizona
Thomas R Taylor, State Director, (602) 967–6265
Paul F Ankney, Assistant State Director, (602) 840–1379

Arkansas
Edward F Mazur, State Director, (501) 394–5724

California
Virgil C Staff, State Director, (510) 524–9446
Vincent H Uhlenkott, State Director, (213) 892–9181
Georgeanne Cifarelli, Assistant State Director, (818) 576–0415
Ruben J Uriarte, Assistant State Director, (510) 247–1968

Colorado
Michael G Curta, State Director
James A Peters, Assistant State Director
State Office: (303) 451–5992

Connecticut
Anastasia Wietrzychowska, State Director, (203) 261–3106

Delaware
Ralph P Flegal, Assistant State Director, (302) 998–5517

Florida
Charles D Flannigan, State Director, (904) 478–0465
G Bland Pugh, Assistant State Director, (904) 932–9406

Georgia
S Christopher Early, State Director, (404) 261–4069
Joye J Pugh, Assistant State Director, (912) 384–9520

Hawaii
Marc Viglielmo, State Director, (808) 373–4856
Richard J Dickison, Assistant State Director, (808) 672–8467

Idaho
Li F Wong, State Director, (208) 924–5716

Illinois
Forest Crawford, State Director, (618) 345–0554
Thaddeus J Lewamdowski, Assistant State Director, (708) 529–8650

Indiana
Jerry L Sievers, State Director, (812) 882–1862

Iowa
Beverly Trout, State Director, (515) 967–6323
Desmond H Bragg, Assistant State Director, (515) 285–1647

Kansas
Thomas H Nicholl, State Director, (913) 642–9320

Kentucky
Jarrett E Washington, State Director, (502) 266–5768
Anne MacFie, Assistant State Director, (606) 663–2800
Ann Petrocelli, Assistant State Director, (502) 259–5542

Louisiana
Walter L Garner, State Director, (504) 766–7207
David Slay, Assistant State Director, (318) 855–4293
George E Sewell, Assistant State Director, (318) 632–2058
Micheal D Sandras, Assistant State Director, (504) 340–0256

Maine
Leland P Bechtel, State Director, (207) 585–2535

Maryland
Bruce S Maccabee, State Director, (301) 271–2307
Thomas B Burch, Assistant State Director, (301) 349–2434

Massachusetts
Joseph P Cambria, State Director, (617) 245–4903

Michigan
William J Murphy, State Director, (517) 394–2320
Linda C Murphy, State Director, (517) 394–2320
Wayne Erickson, Assistant State Director, (313) 534–2293

Minnesota
Richard Moss, State Director, (612) 732–3205
William J McNeff, Assistant State Director, (612) 890–1390

Missouri
Bruce Alan Widaman, State Director, (314) 946–1394
Marvin R Czarnik, Assistant State Director, (314) 625–3941

Mississippi
James A Scarborough, State Director, (601) 748–2473

Montana
Thomas B Danenhower, Assistant State Director, (406) 433–1063

Nebraska
John C Kasher, Board of Directors, (402) 397–7542

Nevada
Alan J Gudaitis, State Director, (702) 459–3774
Sandy Lepore Gudaitis, Assistant State Director, (702) 459–3774

New Hampshire
Peter R Geremia, State Director, (603) 436–9283
Walter E Friesendorf, Assistant State Director, (603) 673–3829

New Jersey
George Filer, State Director, (609) 654–7243
Charles E Ratliff, Assistant State Director, (201) 249–0023

New York
Gary Levine, State Director, (518) 731–9018
Dana M Schmidt, Assistant State Director, (716) 385–3795

North Carolina
P Wayne Laporte, State Director, (704) 882–1732
George E Lund III, Assistant State Director, (704) 366–8340

Ohio
William Edward Jones, State Director, (614) 486–5877
Delbert E Anderson, Assistant State Director, (614) 332–6044
Richard Dell'aquila, Assistant State Director, (216) 524–4919

Oklahoma
Jean Waller-Seifried, State Director, (405) 329–1005
Charles L Pine, Assistant State Director (405) 381–4225

Oregon
Michael R Downey, State Director, (503) 621–3725
Skip D Schultz, Assistant State Director (503) 399–7178

Pennsylvania
Paul G Johnson, State Director, (412) 823–1834

Rhode Island
Daved E Rubien, State Director, (401) 781–1354

South Carolina
William M Hopkins, State Director, (803) 786–9461
Richard M Coffman, Assistant State Director, (803) 776–2948

South Dakota
Ann Deg, State Director, (605) 338–1563
David A Deg, State Director, (605) 338–1563

Tennessee
Leslie Mitts, Assistant State Director, (615) 886–2554

Texas
Ellen R Stuart, State Director, (512) 288–0505
F Joe Lewels, Assistant State Director, (915) 581–0339
Antoinette M Butz, Assistant State Director, (214) 527–1424
Gayle Nesom, Assistant State Director, (713) 772–0222

Utah
Mildred Biesele, State Director, (801) 277–0686
Mara R Ulis, Assistant State Director, (801) 942–0123

Virginia
Mark E Blashak, State Director, (804) 784–3442
Don W Lovett, Assistant State Director, (804) 550–2050

Vermont
Peter R Van Tyle, JD, State Director, (802) 333–4200

Washington
Laurence T Childs, State Director, (206) 488–3805
Gerald E Rowles, Assistant State Director, (509) 327–4868
Sharon D Filip, Assistant State Director, (206) 827–5845

Washington DC
Elaine Douglass, State Director, (202) 232-2410

West Virginia
Theodore R Spickler, State Director, (304) 242-2474
Gregg B Knight, Assistant State Director, (304) 783-5593

Wisconsin
Richard F Thieme, State Director, (414) 351-1450
Jeffery W Sainio, Assistant State Director, (414) 351-0895

New Brunswick, Canada
Stanton Friedman, Provincial Director, (506) 457-0232
Fax: (506) 450-3832

EUROPE

BUFORA - The British UFO Research Association
BM BUFORA
London WC1X 3XX
(01352) 732473
e-mail: mwootten@dial.pipex.com
web: www.bufora.org.uk
The British equivalent of MUFON, with an organizing council, a library, publications, a quarterly magazine, a newsclipping archive, liaison and research directors and a team of field investigators.

CANADA

CUFORN - The Canadian UFO Research Network
77547 592 Sheppard Avenue West
Downsview
Ontario, M3H 6A7
Tel: (416) 787 1905
web: cron-z.mco.on.ca/web/cuform

USA

CAUS – Citizens Against UFO Secrecy
Barry Grenwood
PO Box 176
Stoneham
Massachusetts 02180
e-mail: jan@cyberzone.net

Contact Forum
PO Box 726
Newberg, OR 97132
Tel: 800–366–0264
e-mail: bluewaterp@aol.com

CSETI – The Center for the Study of Extraterrestrial Intelligence
Steven Greer MD
PO Box 15401
Ashville, NC 28813
Tel: 704–254–9650
e-mail: 103275.1472@compserve.com
web: www.cseti.com

CUFOS – The J Allen Hynek Center for UFO Studies
1955 John's Drive
Glenview, IL 60025
Tel: (312) 271 3611
web: cufos.org/index.html
Founded in 1973 by Dr J Allen Hynek who was technical advisor
for the film *Close Encounters of the Third Kind*. Dr Hynek, who is
regarded by many as the father of modern ufology, introduced the
term 'close encounters' into our language. He was a Professor of
Astronomy at Ohio State University when he served as the astro-
nomical consultant to the United States Air Force's Project Blue
Book. He began this work as a sceptic but was persuaded by the
evidence that UFOs were worthy of serious study. CUFOS, which is
based in Chicago, is an international group of scientists, academics,
investigators and volunteers devoted to the examination and study
of UFO phenomena.

FUFOR–Fund for UFO Research
PO Box 277
Mt Rainier, MD 20712
Tel: (703) 684 6032
web: www.fufor.org/

IF – The Intruders Foundation
Budd Hopkins
PO Box 30233
New York, NY 10011
Tel: (212) 645 5278

ISCNI – The Institute for the Study of Contact with
   Non-Human Intelligence
3463 State Street#440
Santa Barbara, CA 93105
Tel: 805–563–8500
e-mail: iscni@aol.com
web: www.iscni.com

NICAP – National Investigations Committee on Ariel Phenomena
10 Linden Street
Congers
NY 10920
e-mail: plawrence@nicap.com
web: www.nicap.com

NICUFO – The National Investigations Committee of UFOs
Dr Frank E Stranges, PhD (President)
14617 Victory Boulevard, Suite 4
PO Box 5
Van Nuys, CA 91411
Tel: (818) 989–5942

OPUS – The Organization for Paranormal Understanding
   and Support
Kathy Hennesy
PO Box 273273
Concord, CA 94527
Tel: (510) 689–2666
web: www.avante-garde.com/opus/

ORTK – Operation Right To Know
PO Box 2911
Hyattsville
Maryland 20784
web: www.galaxy.tradewave.com/editors/mark-hines/ortk.html

PEER – The Program for Extraordinary Experience Research
1493 Cambridge Street
Cambridge, MA 02139
Tel: (617) 497–2667

Project Awareness
PO Box 730
Gulf Breeze, FL 32562
Tel: (904) 432–8888

SSE – The Society for Scientific Exploration
PO Box 3818
University Stations
Charlottesville, VA 22903–0818
Tel: (804) 924–4905

MAGAZINES

Connecting Link
9392 Whitneyville Road SE
Alto, MI 49302–9694
USA

Fate
84 S Wabasha Street
Paul, MN 55107
USA

FSR/Flying Saucer Review
PO Box 162
High Wycombe,
Bucks
HP13 5DZ
England

IUR/International UFO Reporter
2457 West Peterson Avenue,
Chicago, IL 60659
USA

Journal of UFO Studies,
2457 West Peterson Avenue,
Chicago, IL 60659
USA

MUFON UFO Journal,
103 Oldtowne Road
Sequin, TX 78155
USA

Omni,
1965 Broadway
New York, NY 10023–5965
USA

Search Magazine
PO Box 296
Amherst, WI 54406
USA

The Skeptical Inquirer
Box 229
Buffalo, NY 14215
USA

UFO Contact
1b Laulund Vinkelvej 15
Lunde
Denmark

UFO Magazine
PO Box 1053
Sunland
CA 91041
USA

UFO Newsclipping Service
Route 1
Box 220
Plumerville, AR 72127
USA

UFO
1800 South Robertson Boulevard
Box 355
Los Angeles, CA 90035
USA

MUSEUMS

Two of the best known museums devoted to the subject of UFOs are in Roswell, New Mexico. The oldest is the UFO Enigma Museum which is on the south side, close to the airfield where the alien autopsies were witnessed by Glenn Dennis' friend.

The International UFO Museum and Research Center (IUFOMRC), which is in the centre of Roswell, covers 11,000 square feet. In 1996 it received over 70,000 visitors from many countries. The vast majority came to Roswell specifically to visit the museum, as I can affirm, having spoken to many of them during my visit there in July 1996. Watching people pour through the doors of the museum each day is a staggering testament to level of interest that people across the world have in the UFO phenomenon. In many ways the visitors are reminiscent of pilgrims making their way to Lourdes in France or Santiago de Compostela in north-western Spain. Many reported having been 'contacted' in one form or another.

In addition to an extensive array of exhibits and display cases, the museum houses a library and research area. There is also a video room which seats 140 people and runs films throughout the day on an extraterrestrial theme, and a lecture hall that seats 360 people.

IUFOMRC – International UFO Museum and Research Centre
PO Box 2221
114 North Main St
Roswell
NM 88202
Tel: (505) 625 9495
e-mail: IUFOMRC@lookingglass.net
web: www.iufomrc.com

UFO Enigma Museum
PO Box 6047
6108 South Main St
Roswell
NM 88201
Tel: (505) 347 2275

GLOSSARY

AAF Army Air Field. Up to 1947 the US Air Force was known as the Army Air Force. It was an arm of the army, like the infantry and the artillery. On 18 September 1947 it became an independent arm of the defence establishment and was redesignated as the US Air Force. Each airfield was thereafter referred to as an Air Force Base (AFB).

Abduction A CE4 (close encounter of the fourth kind) whereby a person is removed involuntarily to a waiting alien spacecraft or unknown location where he or she is physically, and perhaps mentally, examined and returned to the pick-up point or somewhere nearby. The experience can last for anything between ten minutes and a few hours.

BUFORA The British UFO Research Organization.

CAUS Citizens Against UFO Secrecy.

CE1 Close encounter of the first kind – observation of a UFO within 150 yards.

CE2 Close encounter of the second kind – a sighting of a UFO which leaves some physical evidence, such as a burn mark where it touched the ground.

CE3 Close encounter of the third kind – a sighting of an occupant or entity from a UFO, possibly with some interaction with them.

CE4 Close encounter of the fourth kind – a physical visit to the immediate location of a human being by one or more extraterrestrial, three-dimensional, intelligent beings (ETs), usually for the purposes of communication, education or removal to a UFO craft for specific procedures.

CE5 Close encounter of the fifth kind – this refers to some form of direct communication with an extraterrestrial being, such as in the form of channelling or actual contact or communications.

CSETI The Center for the Study of Extraterrestrial Intelligence.

CSICOP The Committee for the Scientific Investigation of Claims of the Paranormal. It describes the growing interest in 'paranormal' phenomena as an 'apocalypse of unreason', heralding the emergence of a new Dark Age.

CUFOS The J Allen Hynek Center for UFO Studies.

EBE Extraterrestrial Biological Entity – a term used in some US government documents to refer to captured visitors from another world.

Essassani A hybrid species – a genetic cross between earth humans and the greys from Zeta Reticuli.

FOIA The US Freedom of Information Act of 1974 which enables American citizens to gain access to hitherto secret US government documents.

Greys The species of beings said to come from a planet in the star cluster known as Zeta Reticuli. They are generally between 3 feet 5 inches and 4 feet tall, and are said to be the extraterrestrial species responsible for human abductions.

IF Intruders Foundation, founded by Budd Hopkins.

INFO International Fortean Organization.

IUFOMRC International UFO Museum and Research Center.

Merkabah A thought-form vehicle generated by the thought, feelings and energy of individual people. It takes the shape of a star tetra-

	hedron which is made up of two interlocking tetrahedrons. When it spins as a counter-rotating field of energy it can appear as a 'flying saucer' shape.
MJ-12	A committee of 12 senior US military and scientific people, also known as Majestic-12, which controls the policy and activities of the US government with regard to extra-terrestrials and UFOs.
MUFON	The Mutual UFO Network.
NICUFO	The National Investigations Committee on UFOs.
PEER	The Program for Extraordinary Experience Research.
Pleiadian	Pertaining to a cluster of stars known as the Pleiades.
Project Blue Book	An investigation into UFO sightings by the US Air Force, said to have been conducted as a public relations exercise to distract attention from a real investigation being conducted by another agency of the US government.
SSE	The Society for Scientific Exploration.
Third dimension	The dimension in which earthly life functions, at a vibrational frequency of 7.3 cm per second, approximately 2.87 inches per second.
Uriel	The angel who revealed to the prophet Enoch the secrets of the 'workings of heaven, earth and the seas, and all the elements'.
Zeta Reticuli	A group of stars from which the greys are said to come.

BIBLIOGRAPHY

Boylan, Richard, *Close Extraterrestrial Encounters: Positive Experiences with Mysterious Visitors*, Wild Flower Press, Tigard, Oregon, 1994

Brown, Michael F, *The Channeling Zone*, Harvard University Press, Cambridge, Massachusetts, 1997

D'Antonio, Michael, *Heaven on Earth: Dispatches from America's Spiritual Frontier*, Crown Publishers, New York, 1992

Dahl, Lynda, *Ten Thousand Whispers: A Guide to Conscious Creation*, Windsong Publishing, Eugene, Oregon, 1995

Fowler, Raymond E, *The Andreasson Affair: The Documented Investigation of a Woman's Abduction Aboard a UFO*, Prentice-Hall, Englewood Cliffs, New Jersey, 1979, and Wild Flower Press, Newberg, Oregon, 1994

Fowler, Raymond E, *The Andreasson Affair: Phase Two*, Prentice-Hall, Englewood Cliffs, New Jersey, 1982, and Wild Flower Press, Newberg, Oregon, 1994

Fowler, Raymond E, *The Watchers: The Secret Design Behind UFO Abduction*, Bantam Books, New York, 1990

Friedman, Stanton T, *Top Secret/Majic*, Marlowe & Company, New York, 1996

Frissell, Bob, *Nothing In This Book Is True, But It's Exactly How Things Are*, Frog/North Atlantic Books, Berkeley, California, 1994

Good, Timothy, *Beyond Top Secret: The Worldwide UFO Security Threat*, Sidgwick & Jackson, London, 1996

Grosso, Michael, *The Final Choice*, Stillpoint, Walpole, New Hampshire, 1985.

Hall, Richard, *Uninvited Guests: A Documented History of UFO Sightings, Alien Encounters & Coverup*, Aurora Press, Santa Fe, New Mexico, 1988

Hand Clow, Barbara, *The Pleiadian Agenda: A New Cosmology for the Age of Light*, Bear & Company, Santa Fe, New Mexico, 1995

Hopkins, Budd, *Intruders: The Incredible Visitations at Copley Woods*, Ballantine Books, New York, 1987

Hopkins, Budd, *Missing Time*, Ballantine Books, New York, 1981

Hurtak, J J, *The Book of Knowledge: The Keys of Enoch*, The Academy for Future Science, Los Gatos, California, 1977

Jacobs, David, *Secret Life: Firsthand Accounts of UFO Abductions*, Simon & Schuster, New York, 1992

LaVigne, Michelle, *The Alien Abduction Survival Guide: How to Cope with Your ET Experience*, Wild Flower Press, Newberg, Oregon, 1995

Lindemann, Michael, ed, *UFOs and the Alien Presence: Six Viewpoints*, Wild Flower Press, Newberg, Oregon, 1991

Mack, John, *Abduction: Human Encounters with Aliens*, Simon & Schuster, London, 1994

Randles, Jenny and Hough, Peter, *The Complete Book of UFOs: An Investigation into Alien Contacts & Encounters*, Sterling Publishing, New York, 1996

Ring, Kenneth, *The Omega Project: Near-Death Experiences, UFO Encounters, and Mind at Large*, Quill/William Morrow, New York, 1992

Roberts, Jane, The Seth Material, Prentice-Hall, Englewood Cliffs, New Jersey, 1970

Royal, Lyssa and Priest, Keith, *Preparing for Contact: A Metamorphosis of Consciousness*, Royal Priest Research, Phoenix, Arizona, 1993

Thompson, Richard, *Alien Identities: Ancient Insights into Modern UFO Phenomena*, Govardhan Publishing, Alachua, Florida, 1993

Walton, Travis, *The Walton Experience*, Berkeley Publishing Corp, New York, 1978

Readers are invited to communicate with me directly about errors in the text, or to share any information about my next project, which is to document information about children who talk about coming from other worlds. I can be reached by e-mail at *gregory@verinet.com* or by ordinary mail at either of the following addresses:

Suite 450
2 Old Brompton Road
London SW7 3DQ
England

5400 Park Terrace Avenue, 14–102
Greenwood Village,
Colorado, CO 80111
USA

INDEX